THE NAKED ADVISER

GW00976006

AN OPEN GUIDE
TO MONEY

sesame

Published by Sesame Services Ltd.
First Edition. March 2004.

Designed and produced by The Blake Project, Oxford,
www.blakeproject.com, on behalf of Sesame Services Ltd.

The contents of this publication have been based on the
2003–04 tax year.

A CIP record for this book is available from the
British Library.

ISBN 0-9547058-0-7

Foreword

The day I left school, I could recite a treasure trove of obscure Latin verbs. I knew how to warn fellow slaves that Roman soldiers were approaching along the aqueduct, and to put these thoughts into the pluperfect tense.

Unfortunately, this did not help with a host of immediate, practical decisions that faced me, as I entered the adult world from the security and comfort of the parental home. Sesame's 'The Naked Adviser' is our way of helping to fill the gaps that – for one reason or another – the British educational curriculum has never been asked to fill.

Many people find it intimidating and stressful to think about the world of investments, insurance, and retirement planning. In no small part, this is because of the endless jargon the industry has used in the past. The industry has almost created a new language – obscure, confusing, understood only by insiders. Yet many aspects of sound financial planning are nothing more than informed common sense. Sesame is committed to making the world of financial advice more accessible, using straight-talking statements.

An informed public is vital for economic success and personal well-being. We hope this short A–Z guide to the world of money will be seen as a valuable contribution to creating a new climate.

Now if only we could escape those pesky Roman soldiers as easily …

Patrick Gale
Chief Executive
Sesame

Acknowledgements

Thanks are due to the many writers who constantly tackle the muddied world of finance. There's a stream of valuable information out there just waiting to be acted upon, which provided us with an inspirational starting point. Special thanks go to Jim Harris, David Rush and Terry Jones for their support during the painful process of deciphering fact from fiction in this complicated arena. Your staying power must be applauded. Andy Shaw merits a special commendation for making the driest of topics fascinating – your passing quip about statistics earned an affectionate spot in these pages. Thanks also to Liz Light for clearing up the acrimonious topic of divorce, and to the Plain English Campaign, who partly inspired the idea for a no-nonsense guide. You make it look easier than it is. Our thanks also to the learned technical team – Dale, Marcus, Mark, Ian, Neil, Alan, Gemma, Stephen and legal eagle Paul Lockyer for cheering us on, correcting our gaffes and saving us from embarrassment. And to Shelley Robertson of Skandia for sourcing credible statistics so efficiently.

Of course the contributions from some of the UK's leading financial institutions have helped provide an insight into many of the issues of concern to consumers today. So many thanks go to AXA's Louise Barber and Martin Olive, Abbey's Hailey Chan and Neil Jackson, Prudential's Keith Farrell and Graham Taylor, Scottish Widows' Susan Robertson, Jack King and Grant Matheson, Standard Life's Tom Morris, Sandra Kay and Nicola Burton and, last but not least, Zurich's Claire Burton and Paul Hagan.

And many thanks to the pioneering team who met on a Friday afternoon in September 2003 at the Institute of Directors, to think the unthinkable. Among them were Tim Dodd, Ruth Harwood, David McCann (HHM), Maria Miller – good luck in the next General Election, David Radford (Liverpool & Victoria) and Stephen Young.

Finally, thanks to the team who turned the concept into a reality: Sarah Willington, John Hemingway, Kevin Hinton, Jared Aitken, Ian Thomas, Matt Lloyd, Laurence Smith, and Sesame's commercial director, Martin Davis, for his sponsorship and support.

Stuart Gitsham
Editor, March 2004, Sesame

sesame

When looking for expert financial guidance, it's comforting to know that Sesame supports more Independent Financial Advisers (IFAs) than any other company in the UK.

For instance, when you ask your IFA to sift the latest choice of mortgages or pensions or investments, the chances are they'll need Sesame's help – no matter how knowledgeable they are already. That's because Sesame is an IFA membership network. Firms and individual IFAs become members of Sesame and, in return, gain access to a wealth of financial product and service information, support and advice. And if your IFA is a Sesame customer, you'll be pleased to hear that they are among 6,000 others who, together, make Sesame the UK's number one IFA network.

So what's so good about that?

Well, your IFA wants to make sure that he or she is presenting you with the best possible choice based on thoroughly researched advice. Thanks to its size, Sesame has the most widely respected team of researchers in the industry. They constantly monitor the latest financial products and services to enable advisers to access comprehensive online data anytime of the day or night.

What's more, Sesame regulates members' businesses on behalf of the UK's official financial services regulator – the Financial Services Authority (FSA). Sesame works with its members to make sure that the advice they offer and services they provide meet the FSA's stringent regulations: providing regular and comprehensive training, workshops, seminars and publications for its members. So, not only can you be confident that your Sesame IFA is right up to date with the most comprehensive financial information, you can also be sure that they have all the backup of the latest regulatory information and expertise to ensure that the product is right for you.

Next time you meet your financial adviser, ask them which network they belong to. Let's hope they say Sesame.

Features

A

AARDVARK – Well why not? You have to begin somewhere. And money doesn't have to be aard work.

ABI (Association of British Insurers) – represents the collective interests of the UK's insurance industry. The Association speaks out on issues of common interest; helps to inform and participates in debates on public policy issues; and also acts as an advocate for high standards of customer service in the insurance industry. → CONTACTS

ACCIDENT PROTECTION – Would state benefits cover your mortgage and supermarket bills? If not, accident

protection insurance is probably a good idea, especially if you're self-employed.

ACCOUNTANTS – a far from endangered species, mostly harmless, and frequently very useful when dealing with the Inland Revenue.

ACCRUAL RATE – the build-up rate for final salary scheme pensions. If the accrual rate is one sixtieth and you've been a scheme member for 10 years, your pension will be ten sixtieths of your final earnings.

ACCUMULATION UNITS – units held, for example, within a unit trust for investors who don't want to receive income. Instead, income is added to the value of the units. → INVESTMENTS

ACTUARY – a person qualified to calculate insurance risks and premiums.

ADDED YEARS – a pension benefit for final salary schemes allowing members to buy extra years of service.

ADVISER – someone qualified to explain your options and enable you to make an informed decision. → IFA

AER (Annual Equivalent Rate) – shows the return you could expect over a year on a savings or investment account, as if the percentage of interest was rolled up and paid annually. AERs must now be published in all savings advertisements, letting you make better comparisons. → INTEREST RATES

Annuity

What is an annuity?

When you retire, you take the private pension pot you've been building up and buy an annuity from an insurance company. This annuity then pays you a regular income until you die.

- **You don't have to buy your annuity from the provider of your pension.**

- **Shopping around may give you a higher income.**

- **Don't be pressured into a decision – you don't have to buy today.**

- **Once you've bought an annuity you can't change your mind. If interest rates and investment markets are picking up, you may want to delay making the decision, provided you can support yourself.**

- **If you have been paying larger life insurance premiums because of an illness or because you were a smoker, tell your IFA. You may be better off buying an Impaired Life Annuity.**

The companies who sell annuities take a view on how long they think you'll live, and effectively, you hand over your pot in return for a regular income. Rates can, and do, vary. So shop around.

Who needs one?

If you've been paying money into a pension scheme and retirement is here, then you'll have to buy an annuity before you reach 75. Picking the annuity that's right for you could be the most important investment decision of your twilight years.

How much will you get?

Several factors can influence how much you get – your age, health, sex, marital status – and interest rates at the date of your retirement. In recent years, interest rates have been low and so too have annuity rates. A lot also depends on how much risk, if any, you want to take with your income.

Just because you've been saving for your pension with one company, you are not tied to buy your annuity from them. Rates of income on annuities can vary by as much as 25 per cent or more. For one simple example, comparing like-with-like between companies, see the table below.

	Highest annuity	Highest (excluding impaired/enhanced)	Lowest annuity	Weekly difference*
Man aged 60	£7,390	£6,627	£5,565	£35.10
Woman aged 60	£7,680	£6,435	£5,060	£50.39

Best and worst level annuities with no guarantee period for a man and woman aged 60 with a pension pot of £100,000 (www.assureweb.co.uk – December 2003).
* Difference between highest and lowest annuity.

Plus points and pitfalls

As well as different companies, there are different products to choose from. Some carry more risks than others. An Independent Financial Adviser (IFA) will review your complete affairs before directing you towards your best options. What you choose will depend on your personal circumstances.

Is it tax-free?

You can take up to 25 per cent of your personal pension pot (possibly higher for Occupational Pension Schemes) as a tax-free lump sum, but the rest must be used to buy an annuity. The regular income you receive will be liable to tax.

Standard Fixed Income Annuity	No investment risks.	These annuities are more secure. You'll know what your income will be and it will be guaranteed for the rest of your life.
With-Profits Annuity	Investment linked that usually provides a minimum monthly sum.	Could pay you more if your investment fund performs well and exceeds the annual bonus rate on the policy. But it could also pay less if it 'under-performs'.
Unit-Linked Annuity	Not for the faint-hearted. Usually only if you have other sources of retirement income.	If you are prepared to take risks, and don't mind an income that varies, you'll benefit if investment markets rise. Equally, if they drop you could lose out.
Impaired Life and Enhanced Annuity	If your life expectancy is lower than the general population. Where you live may affect rates.	Impaired Life Annuities vary by age and health, but can pay up to 15 per cent more than a conventional annuity. If you are seriously ill, the annual income may reach 80 per cent, against the more usual 6 per cent, of your pension pot. Certain postcodes may receive better rates than others.
Flexible Lifetime Annuity	If you want to pass your pension fund assets onto your estate.	Most annuity assets can't be passed on after death. However, some providers are introducing new 'flexible lifetime' annuity products addressing this.
Income Drawdown	If you want to wait to buy an annuity later, perhaps when the rates are better. Must action by 75 at the latest.	Lets you take money each month from your pension pot and invest the rest. The risk is your pension pot could disappear, and you could live much longer than 75.

The annuity is payable monthly in advance.

For more information about the latest annuity rates speak to your IFA

AGE – one of the first things your IFA needs to know. Never lie.

AIFA (Association of Independent Financial Advisers) – surprisingly enough, the industry body for independent financial advisers. ➔ CONTACTS

AIM (The Alternative Investment Market) – run by the London Stock Exchange as a market for shares in smaller, growing companies, sometimes as a stepping stone for a FTSE listing. ➔ INVESTMENTS

ANNUITY – every pensioner deserves one, the bigger the better. ➔ *Feature*

APR (Annual Percentage Rate) – When you borrow money, every lender is required by law to quote this rate. Always insist on being told the APR, it's the best way of comparing like with like. If a lender can't tell you, find another one.
➔ INTEREST RATES

ARRANGEMENT FEE – a charge made to arrange a loan, covering things like administration and management fees. IFAs are legally bound to disclose their fees, as are stockbrokers.

ASSETS – any property or possession having a value. Most people's major asset is their property, and protection of your assets is key to the maintenance of your wealth. The opposite of liabilities.

AVC (Additional Voluntary Contribution) – an extra payment you can make with tax relief to your company pension scheme, subject to a maximum 15 per cent of your earnings in any tax year. You can pay AVCs to boost your pension pot, which will give you a better pension.

B

BABY BOND – an intended gift from the Government for all children born from 1 September 2002. The aim is to introduce the concept of saving to children. Launch is planned for April 2005, but children won't have access to their fund until the age of 18.

BALLOON PAYMENTS – a lump sum paid during or at the end of a finance agreement to complete a purchase. Commonly used by car retailers.

BANK
"A place that will lend you money if you can prove you don't need it."
Bob Hope

BANKER'S DRAFT – Selling your car and worried that a cheque may bounce? Banker's drafts, prepared by banks or building societies, are secure ways to transfer and receive large sums of money.

BANKRUPTCY – a legal process when an individual is unable to pay his or her debts. The word comes from the bench ('bank') on which Italian money-lenders conducted their business, which was turned over – or 'rupted' – if they failed to meet their commitments.

BARE TRUST – a simple form of trust. The principle is applied to trust funds for children which they are entitled to gain access to on reaching 18. Dividends or interest are treated as taxable income for the parents, making it a less attractive saving vehicle.

BASE RATE – the interest rate set by the Bank of England's Monetary Policy Committee. It is the minimum rate at which banks are prepared to lend money.
→ INTEREST RATES

BEAR MARKET – a term for the stock market going down on a fairly continuous basis, with a steady fall in prices – the opposite to a bull market. 'Bears' tend to be sellers rather than buyers.

BENEFICIARY – the person you leave money or gifts to in your Will, or the person who benefits under a trust.

BIBA (British Insurance Brokers' Association) – the UK independent body for insurance brokers and consumers.

BID OFFER SPREAD – the difference between the buying price and the selling price of stocks and shares.
→ INVESTMENTS

BID PRICE – the price at which you sell stocks and shares or units in a unit trust or other investment.

BILLION – one thousand million, or 1,000,000,000.

> **"If you can count your money, you don't have a billion dollars"**
> *J Paul Getty.*

BILLS – Despite the temptation, it's usually a bad idea to ignore them, especially the red ones. Generally it's easier to manage regular bills by direct debit payments.

BLACK ECONOMY – Not declaring cash-in-hand income on your tax return will incur the wrath of the Inland Revenue. Statistics suggest that in Britain, 5 to 10 per cent of the economy is black. In Italy it's a national sport, averaging nearly 30 per cent.

BLAME – Someone is always responsible, and it could be you. So consider liability insurance.

BLUE CHIP – At the poker table, 'Blue Chips' have the highest value. Blue Chip companies are generally the largest, and also regarded as a safer bet.
→ INVESTMENTS

BONDS – These are offered by governments and corporations. Effectively you lend them a sum of money in return for a fixed rate of interest over a set period of time. At the end, you get back the nominal or face value. In the meantime you can also buy and sell them in the bond markets. → INVESTMENTS

BONUS – what City traders once relied upon to buy their Ferraris. Bonuses are extra payments made by employers or investments. With-profit pension or investment policies may have extra payments added as bonuses.

BOOM – a period of prosperity, to be grabbed with both hands and enjoyed while it lasts. The trick is not to buy at the very top of the market, or you may get burnt on the way back down.

BORROWING – taking a temporary loan of money or assets with the intention of paying it back to the lender, normally with interest.

➜ DEBT, INTEREST RATES, MORTGAGES

BRIDGING LOAN – a short-term, temporary loan often used by property purchasers to bridge the gap between completing the purchase of a property and waiting to complete the sale of a previous property.

BROKE – the state of being penniless.

BROKER – two weeks after broke. The term also means a financial middleman or intermediary.

BUDGET – a financial plan breaking down income against expenditure. The Government produces one every year, as do most businesses. The secret of success is not just to prepare a budget, but to stick to it.

BUILDING INSURANCE – protection against damage to a property, normally your home. ➜ INSURANCE

BUILDING SOCIETY – a financial organisation owned by its members, who are also usually customers. Often referred to as a 'mutual', since the organisation is mutually owned by its members.

BULL MARKET – a term for the stock market going up on a fairly continuous basis, with a steady rise in prices, and the opposite to a bear market. 'Bulls' tend to be buyers rather than sellers.

BUST – the last option after 'twist' and 'stick' in card games, but also what can happen after broke and broker.

BUY-TO-LET – Buyers with enough funds for a deposit can buy properties and rent them out, which pays the mortgage and generates income. Rocketing house prices, and a wide choice of buy-to-let mortgages at low interest rates, have made this a popular investment option.

C

CAPITAL – money or material assets, also known as equity or net worth. In mortgage terms, capital explains the amount outstanding that you owe, not including costs and interest remaining.

CAPITAL GAINS TAX – the tax on the profit made after selling assets such as shares, a business, a second home or a collectable item. Capital loss can be used to offset a capital gain, reducing any tax due.
→ **DIVORCE, TAX TIPS**

CAPITAL GROWTH – an increase in the value of a property, or shares or other assets.

CAPPED RATE MORTGAGES – a mixture of a variable and fixed-rate mortgage. The interest rate doesn't rise above the 'capped' rate during an agreed timeframe.
→ **MORTGAGES**

CASH – A ready supply (or supply of readies) can work wonders when you're negotiating to buy a house or bargaining for a discount.

CASH BACK – a mortgage cash incentive, but if it seems too good to be true, it probably is. Always ask 'what's in it for me?'. Cash back benefits may be cancelled out by other costs such as mortgage transfer fees or expensive insurance. → **MORTGAGES**

CASH FLOW – A strong inflow of cash is good, but too much cash outflow could indicate an underlying problem. Investment analysts examine 'cash flow' to spot a short or long-term cash crisis in a company.

CASH ISA – a risk-free, tax-efficient savings scheme. → **SAVINGS**

CAT – The kitemark for ISAs and mortgages, CAT awards by the Government highlight products that are simple, clear and fair but by no means endorse their suitability for all savers or guarantee performance.

Growing children, growing cost

A baby born in Britain today is likely to cost the parents as much as £140,000[1] by the age of 21. For Ian Thomas of Sesame, sound financial planning is key to dealing with the growing costs of growing.

The recent House of Commons vote on university tuition fees has doubtless left many existing and would-be parents of teenagers feeling worried about how they're going to cope. The current standard fee of £1,125[2] a year seems likely to be replaced with variable fees of up to £3,000[3] a year from 2006–7.

Even without the potential burden of university fees, a baby born in Britain today may cost the parents as much as £140,000 to cover education, food and clothing before he or she reaches 21 – and that's without going wild on designer trainers. In other words, just one child could end up costing you more than most people spend on a family home. So it's critical for parents to feel sure they can meet the monetary demands of their offspring without running up debts themselves.

Barclays[4] estimates that a student at a university outside London who lives away from home will need £3,000

Moneytalk **1**

The bill for parents will continue to rise

to cover living expenses and the new fees of up to £11,236 a year by 2010. Based on this calculation, a student on a three-year course would have a final bill of £33,708.

While loans are available to help students fund their own education, many parents would like to be able to assist their children with these steep costs to avoid them having to start their working life in severe debt.

Don't forget school fees
The biggest bill that some parents may face is for private schooling. School fees usually rise at above the rate of inflation and over the past few years have been increasing at a rate of over 5 per cent a year. Parents who opt to send their child to a private school could be faced with a bill of over £100,000, based on average private school fees of £6,700 per year increasing at 6.7 per cent a year[5]. The secret of paying school fees is to plan early, but even if you have left it late there are investments available to help reduce the financial burden.

Cautious investment makes sense
When it comes to financial planning, spreading the money parents have earmarked for raising their children across a wide range of savings and cautious investment products can make the most sense.

However, over the course of 21 years, a family's financial needs will change considerably. Therefore, it is important to continue to consult your IFA regularly as your children grow older and your financial situation changes.

1. Liverpool Victoria Friendly Society – Cost of a Child (21 Nov 2003)

2. Department for Education and Skills – Aim higher Website (2 Mar 2004)

3. Department of Education and Skills – The Future of Higher Education Student Funding (23 Feb 2004)

4. Barclays – 2010 Graduate Debt Predictions (13 August 2003)

5. Independent Schools Council (2003)

Cards

There is fierce competition between card issuers.

Debit cards take money from your account and pay it to someone else in exchange for goods and services – but only if your account is in credit or within its agreed overdraft limit.

Cash cards are indispensable plastic for extracting money from the 'hole in the wall'. Most can be used in machines other than the issuing bank, but check for withdrawal charges. Some charge up to £1.75 per transaction.

Charge cards are kudos on a card. Unlike credit cards, charge-card members have to clear their balance each month, and usually pay an annual fee for the privilege.

Smart cards are wallet-sized plastic intelligence, offering many potential benefits, and are expected to cut down on card fraud. You'll be able to store financial details, health records, cash and more. But will they be able to load the dishwasher and hoover the house?

But **credit cards** are where the battle to win customers really lies and the 'ace' played is usually lower interest rates, or a limited period of zero rates.

Plastic tactics

Nearly 50 major credit cards offer interest-free deals. So why shell out 18 per cent on an existing card? The trick is, if you can't pay your credit card bill straight away, switch to one with a lower interest rate. The most competitive rates can vary between 9 and 14 per cent. Of course, if you pay your balance in full every month, the interest rate doesn't matter – unless the card charges interest from the day of purchase.

Credit card borrowing represents 4.6 per cent of borrowing, compared to mortgage lending, which equates to 81 per cent of total lending.

40–50 per cent of UK credit card holders repay the balance in full each month. In the USA, this is nearer 60 per cent.

In 2002, we spent £208.7 billion on credit and debit cards in the UK.

A note of caution

If an offer looks too good to be true it usually is. Look out for these catches:

- The 0 per cent may only apply on the balance transferred from another card and not new purchases.

- Some low-interest providers do penalise you if your bill payment is late or you go over the credit limit.

- Check the interest-free period. The best give 56 days between buying something and paying for it. Some cheaper cards do not offer interest-free periods.

- Cards linked to charities may tug at your heartstrings, but generally charge higher rates.

- Spot the retailer store cards labelled 'designer loan sharks'. Use these only to benefit from discounts and pay the balance in full. APRs can climb to as much as 30 per cent, so spreading payments is costly.

- Withdrawing cash or foreign currency using your credit cards will usually be at a higher interest rate.

- Cards that offer fantastic low introductory interest rates will use payments first to clear lower-rate purchases. Once you've cleared your low or nil payments, only then will you start to clear the higher interest rates.

There are of course many positives including free insurance against loss, theft and damage to goods on card purchases, also loyalty schemes offering gifts or Air Miles. The trick is to manage your credit. Choose a card that best suits your lifestyle and regard it as a short-term facility, rather than long-term borrowing.

Debt danger zones

Beware of a growing dependency on your credit cards and balances that continue to grow as the months pass. If you're not disciplined enough to tackle this alone, speak to an IFA who can suggest a suitable course of action. → DEBT

The average UK household today owes more than £6,000 on credit and store cards.

Joseph Williams, a US executive banker, launched the first credit card in 1958, later to be re-named Visa.

CENTRAL BANK – the principal monetary authority of a nation. The setting of interest base rate in the UK rests with our central bank, The Bank of England.

CHAINS – something every house buyer dreads, buying from someone who can't sell until they've found a new home. If one link breaks it will have a knock-on effect.

CHARGE CARD ➔ CARDS

CHARGES – Companies charge for financial services in various ways. IFAs are obliged to disclose how they are paid and how much.

CHARITY – doesn't just begin at home. ➔ TAX TIPS for some charitable gift ideas.

CHILD TAX CREDIT – Is your joint income below £58,000? If so, you could be entitled to Child Tax Credit.
➔ CHILDREN

CHILDREN – a costly venture. ➔ *Feature*

CII (Chartered Insurance Institute) – controlling professional standards in the insurance and financial services industry.

CLAIMS ADVISER/SURVEYOR – sent to assess the damage when you make a significant insurance claim. Remember, they are quantifying the loss for their company, not for you.

CLEARING BANK – commercial banks that use the central clearing house to settle corporate and Government securities for customers and dealers.

CLEARING HOUSE – where cheques and commercial papers are drawn against members' banks and offset so that only the net balances are payable.

CLOSED-ENDED FUNDS – an investment fund with a fixed number of shares issued, such as Investment Trusts. The opposite is an Open-Ended Fund, such as unit trusts, whose number of issued units can vary daily.

CLUSTER POLICY – describes a bundle or 'cluster' of individual contracts, including pensions and life assurance. Each part of the policy or cluster is treated independently for tax and administration purposes and allows you to 'cash in' the benefits separately.

CML (Council for Mortgage Lenders) – a representative body for all members who provide home loans. ➔ CONTACTS

COLLECTIVE INVESTMENTS – a fund that takes money from a number of private investors and pools it together to buy a portfolio of shares to increase the value of their fund. See *Investment Club* and *Unit Trust*.

COMMISSION – the method by which brokers or IFAs are paid by insurance companies for placing business with them. Generally a percentage of the policy premium, commission rates can vary widely.

COMPANY CAR – a perk or a tax nightmare, depending on your usage of the car. ➔ TAX TIPS

COMPANY PENSION SCHEMES – see *Occupational Pension Schemes*.

COMPLETION – when house buyers and sellers breathe a sigh of relief – this is the final legal transfer of keys for cash.

CONTENTS INSURANCE – protection for items in your home and your personal possessions, in case they are lost, stolen or damaged. ➔ INSURANCE

Are you fully covered?

Most of us thankfully will never need to claim to replace all of our contents. But if you do, you'll want to be fully insured. Take the time to assess carefully the cost of replacing all your belongings. Use our checklist as a guide.

- ☐ Carpets, floor coverings
- ☐ Curtains, blinds, fittings
- ☐ Lighting
- ☐ Pictures, ornaments
- ☐ Antiques, collectables

Living rooms:
- ☐ Soft furnishings
- ☐ Furniture
- ☐ TV, DVD, video, stereo
- ☐ Games console, games
- ☐ Telephones, answerphone
- ☐ Computer, software

Dining room:
- ☐ Table and chairs
- ☐ Furniture
- ☐ Cutlery
- ☐ China, glassware

Kitchen/utility:
- ☐ Kitchen units, furniture
- ☐ Oven, cooker
- ☐ Fridge, freezer
- ☐ Dishwasher
- ☐ Washing machine
- ☐ Tumble dryer
- ☐ Kitchenware, utensils
- ☐ Electrical appliances
- ☐ Vacuum cleaner

Bedrooms:
- ☐ Beds, furniture
- ☐ Linen, bedding

Bathrooms:
- ☐ Fixtures and fittings
- ☐ Furniture
- ☐ Towels etc.

Garage and garden:
- ☐ DIY equipment, tools
- ☐ Lawnmower
- ☐ Garden furniture
- ☐ Garden tools
- ☐ Play equipment
- ☐ Plants

Personal belongings:
- ☐ CDs, DVDs, videos
- ☐ Books, toys
- ☐ Computer games
- ☐ Wines, spirits, provisions
- ☐ Photographic equipment
- ☐ Jewellry, watches
- ☐ Musical instruments
- ☐ Clothes, accessories
- ☐ Anything else?

Children

The costs of raising a child are variously estimated between £50,000 and £300,000. The case for financial planning is obvious, and gives family planning a whole new meaning.

Bare essentials

- **Arrange life and income protection as a priority.**

- **Write or update your Will to reflect your new wishes.**

- **Start setting aside regular amounts for your child's future.**

- **Explain the tax advantages to grandparents of cash gifts.**

- **Consider how you will help fund the rising costs of a university education.**

Ten tips for survival

1. Think ahead
If both parents currently work, consider how you'll cover the potential loss of a second income or pay for childcare, and still pay all the essential bills. Could you start to set aside a regular sum from a second salary, perhaps into a Cash ISA or savings account?

2. Claim any benefits
Parents have an array of benefits available, depending on circumstances. These include Child Benefit, Child Tax Credit, Working Tax Credit and Maternity Grants.

3. Protection first, savings second
Protect your life and income before you start saving. Parental priorities should be:
- Life insurance
- Income protection cover
- Health insurance
- Savings and investments.

4. Saving for a head start
Parents are entitled to Child Benefit for each child until they reach 18. Earmarking this to set up life cover and investments for your children can prevent this being absorbed into your household income. You may also be entitled to Child Tax Credit.

5. Investing for children
Investing for your child's future is one of the best gifts you can make.
- Children's Bonus Bonds from National

Savings and Investments – the Government-backed bank – are five-year, fixed-rate lump sum plans. The minimum investment is £25, the maximum £1,000.

• Friendly Societies offer tax-exempt saving schemes called Children's Bonds.

• Premium Bonds can be cashed at only eight days' notice. The minimum investment is £100, the maximum £30,000. Average return is 2.4 per cent.

• Invest in unit trusts or open-ended investment companies (OEICs). Some are packaged to appeal to parents looking for a child-focused investment, with minimum monthly savings of £20. There are thousands of funds to pick from – you can opt for either growth or income investments.

6. The child-friendly tax man
By opening a deposit account in a child's name, parents can avoid paying tax. Fill in Inland Revenue form IR85 so that interest is paid tax free. If a minor unmarried child's gross interest exceeds £100 a year, the whole amount will be taxed as if it belonged to you, the parent.

Children also have a tax-free allowance of £4,615 a year before any tax on income is charged to the child.

Investments that aim for capital growth can also be tax efficient. Children have their own annual capital gains tax exemption, so can profit on any sale up to £7,900 and pay no tax, even if the parents gave them the original capital.

Children can also reduce grandparents' Inheritance Tax (IHT) liabilities. Grandparents may give as much as they like and no IHT

is payable – provided the grandparents live for seven years after the gift.

If you're giving away large sums to your child or grandchild but want to maintain control, consider the benefits of a trust fund.

7. Pension gift for the long term
Investing in a stakeholder pension scheme is another tax efficient saving vehicle. Parents and grandparents can take out a stakeholder pension for the children, investing a maximum of £2,808 in each tax year, which is topped up by the Government to £3,600 with basic rate tax relief.

8. School fees
Private schooling is expensive and fees could amount to £150,000. More people are considering flexible mortgages for school fees planning, drawing an income against their home.

9. University fees
While private education is a personal choice, university education is likely to find a place in your list of long-term saving aims. Barclays has estimated that, by 2010, a graduate leaving university will carry a debt of up to £34,000. There are many tax-free saving plans and investments available.

10. Write a Will
Make your wishes known in a legal Will including guardianship arrangements for your children in case both parents die.
➔ WILLS

CONTRACT – a legal agreement between a buyer and a seller. It doesn't always involve signing a piece of paper, so beware.

CONTRACTING IN / OUT OF S2P – Members of an occupational pension scheme are usually contracted out of S2P (State Second Pension, the replacement for SERPS, the State Earnings Related Pension Scheme, since April 2002). But holders of personal pensions can also use their plans to contract out of S2P. Confused? That's not surprising. Consult an IFA who can calculate whether you should contract in or out. It depends on your age, earnings and attitude to risk.

CONVEYANCE – When buying a house, the conveyancing process establishes exactly what you're buying, checks all the legal documents, including title deeds, and carries out searches before completion. Best left to a solicitor or specialist conveyancer, unless you're a legal eagle.

COOLING OFF – time to change your mind about an investment or insurance, also known as a cancellation period. Usually 14 days but not all products offer this benefit.

CORPORATE BONDS – issued by companies as a way of raising funds and usually repaid with interest at half-yearly intervals. The more risky are sometimes labelled Junk Bonds or High-Yield Bonds. ➜ INVESTMENTS

CORPORATION TAX – the tax paid by limited companies on their profits.

COUNCIL TAX – based on the value of a domestic property and used to fund local council services. If you have just bought a property and you believe the valuation banding (between A and H) is wrong, you have six months to appeal.

COVENANT – a promise written into deeds, mortgages and other financial contracts, which you must stick to or you're in danger of being in breach of your agreement and you may face the prospect of penalty charges.

CREDIT CARD ➜ CARDS

CREDIT INSURANCE – payment protection for credit or loan repayments if you are sick or lose your job.

CRITICAL ILLNESS INSURANCE – a lump sum paid if you are diagnosed with a specific serious illness. Most policies cover cancer, heart disease, kidney failure and strokes plus a handful of other conditions. But you won't be paid anything if you suffer from an illness that is not on the list, so always check the policy carefully. ➜ HEALTH INSURANCE

D

DAY TRADERS – people who buy and sell within the same day to try to make quick profits on movements in share prices, using the Internet. Day trading can lead to nightmares.

DEATH AFTER RETIREMENT BENEFITS – the pension and lump sum paid to a deceased member's spouse and/or other dependants.

DEATH BENEFIT – the payout on a life insurance policy, to protect those you care about from financial loss. It's extremely sensible if you have a mortgage, and a partner or children financially dependent on you. ➜ LIFE INSURANCE

DEATH IN SERVICE BENEFITS – If someone dies while still employed and before retirement, this is the pension and lump sum paid to their spouse and/or dependants. It's important to keep your 'expression of wish' forms up to date.

DEBIT CARD ➜ CARDS

DEBT – You can never have too much money, but you can have too much debt. ➜ *Feature*

DEBTOR – a name given to those who owe money. Even countries can be debtors.

DECREASING TERM ASSURANCE – life insurance for a specific duration, where the sum the policy will pay out gets smaller over time. This is usually sold with a repayment mortgage to cover the steady reduction in the money owed.
➜ LIFE INSURANCE

DEEDS – when signed, sealed (quite literally) and delivered during the completion phase of a house purchase, the title in the property passes to the new owner.

DEFAULT – failure to meet a financial commitment, especially payment on a loan or mortgage. Generally, if a monthly mortgage payment is not received thirty days after the due date, the mortgage is in default.

Debt

Most people, at some point in their lives, have some form of debt. The average household owes more than £6,000 on credit and store cards alone, and some pay more each month on credit cards than on their monthly mortgage.

Should you be worried about your own level of debt? This depends upon your philosophy towards life, your dependency on borrowing, and the overall balance between what you owe and what you own. There are no right or wrong answers, but debt can become a very heavy burden.

Breaking the debt cycle

To get your finances into shape, complete a monthly budget planner to see exactly where your money is going. If you are heading into the red, you will need to start making some decisions to curb spending. Look out for:

• Household bills. Changing providers for gas, electricity and phone can save hundreds of pounds each year.
• Credit cards offering lower interest rates and introductory zero rates.
• Savings by direct debit. Most utility companies now provide them.
• Options to clear non-mortgage debt once and for all, perhaps using the equity you have in your house or an investment bonus.
• Review your protection policies. Can you arrange effective but cheaper cover elsewhere? Check also that you're not doubling up on cover.

Also look at the various APRs you're being charged on credit. Minimise the interest you are paying by tackling the highest first and work your way down. Depending on how stretched you are, it may be prudent to switch card providers or clear credit card debt (which is typically much higher) with a lower APR loan. Consider then removing the temptation by cutting up your cards and sticking to cash purchases.

Bare essentials

■ **Store cards have notoriously high APRs.**

■ **Avoid spending to your full credit card limit. Many companies just keep raising it. If the temptation is too great, ask the credit provider to reduce your limit.**

■ **Don't assume that rising house equity means you can afford more debt. Appreciate that using some equity to clear debt is simply spreading it over a longer term.**

■ **Flat rates can be deceptive and are not to be confused with fixed rates. Basically, you pay the interest rate on the initial loan for the entire term. → INTEREST RATES**

■ **Don't rely on winning the lottery – it's one of the longest shots in gambling.**

What can I do if my debt has reached crisis point?

Don't panic; get your IFA to examine the situation, recommending the best approach. The Consumer Credit Counselling Service and National Debtline can also offer practical advice. If your bank balance is looking the worse for wear, contact your bank manager to discuss options. → CONTACTS

Controlling your spending is a step in the right direction. Your IFA can give you more tips on budgeting and debt control.

"Annual income twenty pounds, annual expenditure nineteen nineteen six, result happiness.

Annual income twenty pounds, annual expenditure twenty pounds ought and six, result misery."

Mr Micawber (Charles Dickens).

Check your debt risk with a simple monthly budget

Monthly income £		Petrol		Optional spending	
Take home pay		Road Tax and MOT		Credit/store cards	
Maintenance income		Car maintenance		Entertainment	
Government benefits		Car insurance		Club memberships (gym etc)	
Investment income		Commuting costs			
TOTAL INCOME		Other transport (taxi fares etc)		Newspapers and magazine subs	
		Food		Socialising	
Monthly outgoings £		Pets		Cigarettes	
Fixed costs		Childcare		Clothes	
Mortgage/rent		School fees		Holidays/travel	
Endowment policies		Children activities (clubs etc)		Gifts – birthdays and seasonal occasions	
Gas		Telephone line rental		TOTAL OUTGOINGS	
Electricity		Telephone bills			
Water		Mobile phone		TOTAL INCOME	
Council tax		Life assurance		minus	
Buildings & Contents insurance		Health insurance		TOTAL OUTGOINGS	
TV licence		Medical costs		TOTAL	
Car rental or loan payments		Loan repayments			

DEFERRED PAYMENT – an agreed period of time before an insurance company will pay any benefit, which usually applies to injury or illness claims.
➜ HEALTH INSURANCE

DEFINED BENEFIT SCHEME – also known as a Final Salary Scheme.
➜ PENSIONS

DEFINED CONTRIBUTION SCHEME – also known as a Money Purchase Pension Scheme. ➜ PENSIONS

DEFLATION – when there's a sustained period of falling prices, and the opposite to inflation, when prices rise.

DEL-BOY – There's a touch of Del in all of us – "This time next year we'll be millionaires!"

DEPOSIT – a down payment on a property or item to secure it against other purchasers. Usually calculated as a percentage of the purchase price.

DEPRECIATION – the fall in value of an asset. Treat yourself to a new car, and it will depreciate in value the minute you leave the garage forecourt.

DERIVATIVES – come in many shapes and sizes, with names like futures, options, and warrants. On the whole, these are only for professionals, who use derivatives to reduce risks for investors. Traders in derivatives can make or lose vast sums of money – that's what happened to the infamous Nick Leeson who bankrupted Barings Bank.

DIRECT DEBIT – an automated way of making regular payments to organisations and service providers, which can help simplify control of monthly outgoings.

DISCLOSURE – to reveal or make information known. IFAs and tied agents must 'disclose' the level of commission they will earn from selling financial products. Consumers are also obliged to disclose the whole truth when filling in insurance proposals.

DISCOUNTED MORTGAGES – a special deal to lure borrowers, usually a guaranteed discount on the standard variable rate for a set period.
➔ MORTGAGES

DISCRETIONARY BROKER – a busy investor's right hand man or woman, with written authority to invest money on the client's behalf, following an agreed set of goals and investment tactics.
Trust is vital. ➔ IFA

DIVERSIFICATION – spreading the risk, hedging your bets, not putting all your eggs in one basket. ➔ INVESTMENTS

DIVIDEND – part of a company's profits paid to the people who own shares in it. This pay-out is never guaranteed and the amount received will vary, depending on performance and future expansion plans.

DIVORCE ➔ *Feature*
"For a while we pondered whether to take a vacation or get a divorce. We decided that a trip to Bermuda is over in two weeks, but a divorce is something you always have."
Woody Allen

DOG – a poor investment. Financial newspapers often publish 'Dogs & Stars'.

DOW JONES – the Dow Jones Industrial Average. 'The Dow' is an index of the New York Stock Exchange, a basket of thirty shares that give an even indication of the general market.

DUTY – a Government tax on imports or exports, largely eliminated on trade between European Union countries. If you have a partner or children, many would argue you have a duty to organise your finances.

Divorce

Suddenly solo

For couples making a clean break, finances can be a thorny issue. Suddenly, the money that has paid for one household needs stretching for two.

Parting company amicably eases the financial pressure – lawyers' fees can severely dent your finances. Here are a few ideas to smooth the process.

Unravelling outgoings and assets

First, add up all your outgoings taking into account your entire household, family and personal spending. Make another list for the additional costs of living separately – house, a second car, household expenses and insurance.

Next list all your assets, including your joint possessions – house, car and savings – as well as personal assets like pensions

and investments. See if you can agree how to split these and meet the costs of living independently. Inherited money must also be added to the assets pot, unless it's in a specific trust. Before divorcing, utilise your capital gains tax allowance by transferring assets.

Home alone

The reality is that few can afford to shoulder a mortgage alone, so downsizing becomes the only option. Sometimes a wife may be awarded the property instead of a share of the husband's pension.

Remember, a joint mortgage remains the responsibility of both parties, even after separation.

Pension rights

The landmark date, 1 July 1996, meant partners applying for divorce were entitled to a share of their spouse's pension. Applying to either sex, and covering occupational, personal and stakeholder pensions, the courts may either offset it against another asset – like the property – or earmark (set aside) a tax-free lump sum and/or income for the partner. The main disadvantage of earmarking is if your ex-spouse dies or you re-marry, the pension or annuity is lost.

Latest rules allow part of a member's pension scheme benefits to be placed in the ex-spouse's name, giving the receiver complete control over the fund. It's usually up to the recipient whether they keep it in the same scheme, or transfer it to an approved pension scheme. There is no restriction on the percentage, provided the Courts sanction it. The benefit is kept even if your ex-spouse dies or you re-marry.

Seek advice from an IFA who specialises in pension splitting.

Bank accounts
It's sensible to close joint credit cards and accounts, as you are both liable for any overdraft. Make sure you inform companies of your new account details and transfer direct debit arrangements.

Insuring your new start
Financial security is even more important now. As well as transferring home and car insurance policies into your name, remember you need to cover your mortgage payments with a single life insurance policy.

What about insuring maintenance payments? Confidential life insurance policies can secure this income if the partner providing maintenance dies. Also, if you are working to replace missing income, some form of disability insurance is an extra safeguard. ➜ LIFE INSURANCE

Wills
It is prudent to review any Will and for both parties to draft new ones. Divorce does not invalidate any current Will. Without a Will your husband or wife will automatically inherit some or all of your estate until your divorce is finalised.
➜ WILLS

Do Common Law Marriages receive the same entitlements as married couples?
They do not exist in England and Wales (although Scotland recognises marriages 'by custom and repute'). This means no entitlement to maintenance, although child support is still payable. If one partner owns the home the other has to prove they effectively contributed financially. Seek a solicitor's advice immediately.

Are pre-nuptial agreements always upheld in court?
The courts may take them into account, but this isn't a legally binding contract.

If you sell an endowment policy, will you make more than by surrendering it?
You will usually make more money but this isn't always the case. Get advice from your IFA first.

As a single working parent, are you entitled to any extra income support?
You may be entitled to Working Tax Credit.

As the homeowner, do you still have to pay the full council tax bill?
If there is just one adult in the home, you can claim a reduction of 25 per cent off your bill.

E

EARLY REDEMPTION – If you borrow money and pay it back before the end of the loan term, the lender will lose the interest they expected to charge. So early redemption may involve a charge to you, if this was agreed as one of the conditions.

EARNINGS – in company accounts, what's left as net profit for the shareholders after interest and tax has been deducted.

EARNINGS CAP – for certain occupational pension schemes and personal pensions, the maximum amount of salary that an individual employee can use as the basis for contributions to their pension scheme. The Chancellor of the Exchequer reviews the amount every year in the Budget. ➔ PENSIONS

EARNINGS PER SHARE (EPS) – the earnings of a company, divided by the number of ordinary shares issued, and normally calculated in pence.

ECONOMISTS – experts in the study of production, consumption and the management of wealth and resources.

EMERGENCY FUND – Could you get hold of cash quickly to deal with an emergency? ➔ SAVINGS

EMERGENCY TAX CODE – If there's some delay calculating your correct tax code for Pay As You Earn (PAYE) the Inland Revenue will issue a temporary or emergency tax code.

EMPTY NESTERS – According to marketing gurus, these are parents with spare time and spare money because their children have grown up and left home. It shows what little the gurus know.

ENDOWMENT – a life insurance and savings policy that pays a specified lump sum on death – and often critical illness – during a fixed term, normally between 10 and 25 years. If the insured survives for the full term a cash amount is payable, but the amount is not guaranteed.

EQUITIES – another term for ordinary shares in companies. ➔ INVESTMENTS

EQUITY – For homeowners, equity is the difference between the market value of the property and the amount still owed on the mortgage. So, effectively, the equity in your house is what you own, and your mortgage company owns the rest. If the mortgage is bigger than the current value of the home, the difference is called 'negative equity'.

EQUITY HOUSING – an arrangement by which a person part-owns a property, with the balance being owned by a Housing Association. If the value of the property has increased by the time it is sold, the individual gets their share of the increase in value.

EQUITY RELEASE – a process for homeowners to get cash out of their property. This may be by taking out an increased mortgage, or an additional loan, based on an up-to-date valuation of the property. For older homeowners, there are arrangements by which they can give up part of their ownership, in return for cash, with the lender being repaid when the property is sold on the death of the homeowner.

ESTATE – a term for the total value of all your assets, usually only added-up after death. ➔ WILLS

ESTATE PLANNING – a fancy term for trying to organise your assets to reduce the Inheritance Tax that may be due on death. ➔ WILLS

ETHICAL FUNDS – If you want to invest in a company that's not considered to be involved in 'anti-social' activities, you'll need to look at listings of Ethical Funds. Some funds avoid companies with a poor environmental record; others shirk manufacturers of weapons or tobacco products.

EURO – European single currency, introduced on 1 January 2002.

Twelve Member States in the European Union have adopted the single currency:

- Austria
- Ireland
- Belgium
- Italy
- Finland
- Luxembourg
- France
- Portugal
- Germany
- Spain
- Greece
- The Netherlands

Denmark and UK have opt-out clauses, which imply that they are not obliged to adopt the euro. Sweden will join the euro zone as soon as it has fulfiled all the conditions.

EXCESS – the share of a loss you pay if you make an insurance claim. Usually, the higher the excess, the lower the premium. ➔ INSURANCE

EXCHANGE – another word for a market, such as Stock Exchange.

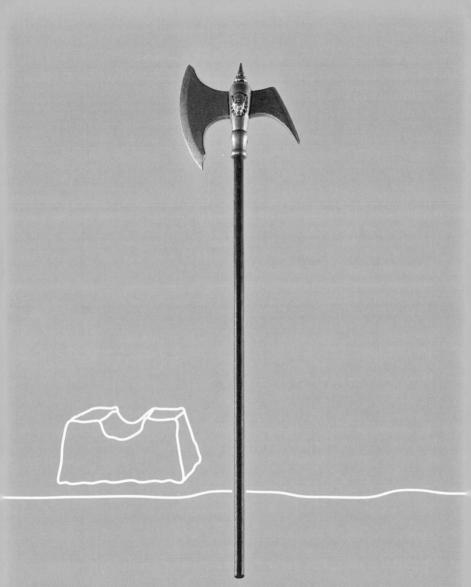

EXCHEQUER – the UK Government department, commonly referred to as the Treasury, and run by the Chancellor of the Exchequer.

EXCISE DUTY – a special form of tax charged when certain products are sold. Fuel and alcohol are where Customs and Excise earn their biggest wedge.

EXECUTION-ONLY SERVICE – an arrangement for buying and selling shares, but not offering advice. These services simply do what you instruct them. ➜ **IFA**

EXECUTOR – specified in your Will as the person or organisation you have appointed to administer your estate and to distribute the assets to the beneficiaries after your death. The Executor can be a relative or friend, or a professional such as a solicitor or a bank manager who will charge for the service.

EXPECTATIONS – invariably Great. Is it better to have modest expectations and be pleasantly surprised, or to be wildly optimistic and then disappointed?

EXPENSES – Nothing comes for free, and it is important to understand how the costs that, say, insurance investment companies incur are recovered from investors. All investment companies have to disclose their expenses, which will be deducted from the return they make, before they pass on the balance to you, as an investor.

EXPERTS – Some may say they're ten a penny. Bona fide experts have detailed knowledge that might help you in making decisions. ➜ **IFA**

EXPRESSION OF WISH – If you have a pension, you'll need to keep this form up-to-date. Also known as a nomination form, it indicates who should receive any lump sum death benefit. It is not necessarily binding as Executors are entitled to exercise discretion if they deem it necessary. Speak to your pension provider or HR department to check yours.

EXTENDED WARRANTY – an insurance policy on goods you may buy, giving a further period of warranty (guarantee) after the manufacturer's warranty has expired. Always read the small print to check what is covered, and what you might have to pay in the event of a claim.

F

FACE VALUE – also known as the nominal or par value. For a bond, it is the amount that will be paid when the bond is redeemed at the end of its life.

FANTASY INVESTMENT – Play the game without actually making or losing real money – a good way to teach yourself how to trade in stocks and shares.

FAT CATS – corporate executives who, on the face of it, are overpaid and underworked – especially if their pay is not directly linked to the performance of the company.

FINAL SALARY SCHEME – a pension arrangement provided by some employers, where the pension is related to the salary received when the employee ceases employment. The pension will increase with the number of years spent in the pension scheme, on a formula, subject to any limits set by the Inland Revenue. ➜ PENSIONS

FINANCIAL ADVISER ➜ IFA

FINANCIAL OMBUDSMAN SERVICE – a public body that can help with most financial complaints from the public, replacing a number of different ombudsmen who dealt with financial firms. ➜ CONTACTS

FIRM PRICE – the basis on which shares are normally traded on the London Stock Exchange, where a market maker has to hold to a price quoted to a broker or another market maker.

FISCAL POLICY – another term for the Government's policies on taxation and spending.

FIXED INTEREST – the general term to describe bonds, because they produce a pre-determined income, in contrast with other investments, such as equities.

FIXED-RATE MORTGAGES – mortgages with an interest rate fixed for a set period, usually between one and ten years. If the mortgage is repaid before the

end of the agreed period, there may be a penalty charge. See *Early Redemption*
→ MORTGAGES

FIXTURES (AND FITTINGS) – items that are usually nailed or screwed to the walls, ceilings or floors, and transferred on the sale of a property.

FLEXIBLE MORTGAGES – If you're feeling flush, flexible mortgages allow you to pay more each month to reduce the mortgage, or to pay less when cash is tight (subject to conditions).
→ MORTGAGES

FLOTATION – the process by which a limited company has its shares introduced on to a stock market for the first time.

FORM 53 – When you receive your Form 53, it's time to crack open the 'Bolly'. This is documentary proof that your mortgage has been paid off, confirming that the property owner has a clean title.

FORTUNE – favours the brave, and shrewd investors hopefully manage to amass one.

FREE – There's 'no such thing as a free lunch'. So always ask yourself why a financial offer is described as free. Is the person making the offer expecting or getting something in return?

FREEHOLD – ownership of a property without any obligation to others. See also *Leasehold*.

FRIENDLY SOCIETY – a form of mutual organisation set up for the benefit of its members. Many friendly societies date back to the 1800s. A friendly society does not have shareholders who expect to receive the benefit of any profits. See *Building Society* and *Mutual Society*.

FROZEN PENSIONS – don't actually exist, but it's a common way of describing a 'Deferred Pension'. This is an Occupational Pension Scheme that is held in your name when you leave an employer and continues to grow on your behalf as invested funds earn income.
→ PENSIONS

FSA (Financial Services Authority) – the independent regulator overseeing all the providers of financial products and services. It licenses these organisations, and ensures that they all operate in an acceptable manner. **→ CONTACTS**

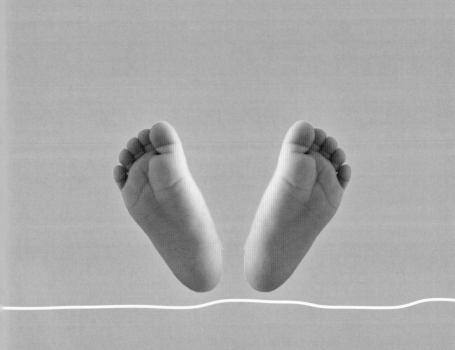

FSAVCS (Free Standing Additional Voluntary Contributions) – extra payments which members of an occupational pension scheme can make to boost their pension pot. ➔ PENSIONS

FTSE 100 – Investors can play the FTSE, as well as play footsie. The FTSE 100 is an index which measures the performance of Britain's biggest companies by market capitalisation. It's calculated by FTSE International, part owned by the Financial Times and the London Stock Exchange, and the companies included in the top 100 are reviewed every quarter. The index was set at 1,000 points when it was launched in January 1984, and reached its high point of 6,930.2 on 30 December 1999. The companies that make up the FTSE 100 are regarded as 'Blue-Chip'.

FTSE 100 – then and now

January 2004 saw the 20th anniversary of the FTSE 100 index. Compare the top five.

1984	market capitalisation £bn
1 British Petroleum	7.4
2 Shell Transport & Trading	6.4
3 General Electric Co	4.9
4 Imperial Chemical Industries	3.9
5 Marks & Spencer	2.8
2004	
1 BP	100.6
2 HSBC	97.6
3 Vodafone	95.2
4 GlaxoSmithKline	77.3
5 Royal Bank of Scotland	48.5

Source: Financial Times and FTSE Group (www.ftse.com)

FUND MANAGER – a professional investor who buys and sells investments to make up a portfolio, which other investors can buy into. A good fund manager will choose investments that perform better than the overall market over time. However, past performance is no guarantee of future performance.

FUNDS – cash in hand, but also describes an investment vehicle where money is pooled together. Pension schemes will invest their pension assets in funds (referred to as institutional funds). There are also retail funds that are made available to the individual investor.
➔ INVESTMENTS

FUNERAL – When your day comes, you'll no longer need to worry about money. But an average funeral costs £2,000 – a nasty surprise to leave behind, unless you make financial plans for the event.

FURBS (Funded Unapproved Retirement Benefit Scheme) – a 'pension' arrangement put in place, for senior managers, which does not qualify for favourable tax treatment. It is normally used for individuals whose salary exceeds the earnings cap, or where the period of service will be very short.

FUTURES – a contract to buy or sell something at a fixed price in the future. It was originally used for the sale or purchase of commodities, where the producer or user wanted to have some certainty on the price.

G

GAMBLERS ANONYMOUS – a self-help organisation, set up in 1957, to help people addicted to gambling. Caution: 'Gambling can seriously affect your wealth'.

GAZUMPING – when someone bids higher for a property after the seller has accepted your bid. Surveys show one in ten house buyers gazump rivals to secure a property. There is no legal redress. (The sealed bids system in Scottish Law means that buyers in Scotland neatly avoid gazumping.)

GDP (Gross Domestic Product) – the total market value of all goods and services produced each year within the borders of a country. It's used as a basic measure of growth and relative wealth. The GDP per Capita, obtained by dividing the total GDP by the population, is a more meaningful indicator of prosperity, but excludes the Black Economy.

GEARING – the ratio between your borrowings/debt and your assets. In property terms, if your house is valued at £100,000 and your outstanding mortgage is £50,000, your gearing is 50 per cent.

GILTS – UK Government bonds or securities issued to raise public funds. Because they are Government-backed they are usually safe and secure, hence 'gilt-edged'. The stocks are mostly fixed interest but some are index-linked.

GLAMOUR STOCK – an 'in vogue' stock that's thrust into the spotlight because of good returns or it's in a trendy investment sector.

GNP (Gross National Product) – the total value of goods and services produced each year by a country. Similar to GDP (Gross Domestic Product), but includes the net income received from other countries.

GOLD – a desirable commodity that once fixed the value of currency exchange rates (the Gold Standard). Although this is no longer the case, gold remains a prized possession and is actively traded on commodity markets.

GRADUATE – someone who holds a degree from a university or college and in all probability, a mass of debt. It's estimated that by 2010, the average graduate debt will be up to £34,000.

GROSS – the total, without deductions. For example, Gross Earnings = earnings before stoppages for tax, NI and other deductions.

GROUND RENT – Owners of leasehold properties pay this annual fee to the freeholder covering maintenance and servicing.

GROUP PERSONAL PENSION – an arrangement made, often by smaller companies, so employees can join a personal pension on a group basis.

GUARANTEED CAPITAL BONDS – designed for cautious investors who sacrifice some of the stock market gains in return for accepting none of the stock market losses.
→ INVESTMENTS

GUARANTEED INCOME BONDS – a National Savings income bond that provides a level and fixed monthly income, but for pensioners only. Also known as Pensioner Bonds.

GUARANTOR – a person who agrees to cover a debt for someone else if repayments can't be met. Typically, parents often agree to guarantee first mortgages for children who are finding their salaries are too small to get onto the property ladder. Guarantors accept legal responsibility for any shortfall or non-payment.

H

HAZARDS – make insurers nervous. So if you're obsessed with adrenaline rushes, check that your extreme pastime is not excluded under any policies you take out – and be prepared to pay extra.

HEALTH → HEALTH INSURANCE

HEDGING – best carried out in early spring if you're a gardener. But for financial pruning, this is a tactic to thin out investment risks by spreading them. Without hedging, investors risk over exposure to a downturn in one specific commodity or sector.

HIDDEN CHARGES – costs tucked away in the small print, where they remain well and truly hidden. Good eyesight alone will not do. You also need a sharp brain and dogged tenacity to plough through the 'terms and conditions' that hide the hidden charges.

HIGH YIELD BONDS – also known as Junk Bonds, but sales people prefer High Yield – it sounds far more polite for these riskier bonds. → INVESTMENTS

HIRE PURCHASE – buying goods by paying a regular monthly sum. Under the terms of a Hire Purchase (HP) agreement, the goods being sold remain the property of the owner (seller) until the hirer (purchaser) has made the final payment.

HOME – may be where your heart is, but also a place where many elderly parents end up, often at a cost which nobody anticipated.

HOME INCOME PLANS – a plan to release equity in the home without selling it. Used to generate some income as an alterative for elderly people who are 'asset rich but cash poor.'

HOSPITAL CASH PLANS – health insurance policies that pay out a tax-free sum for each day you are treated as an in-patient or day-patient at a NHS or private hospital. They can include cash payments for other medical treatments, such as dental treatment and chiropody, but should not be confused with private medical insurance. → HEALTH INSURANCE

HUNGER – without it, there'd be no need for this guide.

Health Insurance

Who needs health insurance?
With state support largely focused on emergency treatment, health protection has become increasingly important. Illness is never planned, often striking at a critical time. If you're self-employed or supporting a family, having this financial safety net can alleviate worries and speed up medical treatments.

What choices do I have?
There are four main product areas:

Private Medical Insurance – pays for quicker treatment of curable, short-term medical conditions at a time and place to suit.

Critical Illness Insurance – a benefit to help with expenses and loss of income if you are diagnosed with a serious illness. Paid as a tax-free lump sum or monthly income.

Income Protection Insurance (also known as Permanent Health Insurance or Long Term Disability Insurance) – picks up where sick pay (if any) leaves off, giving you a regular income until you recover.

Long-Term Care Insurance – a benefit providing funds for part or full-time care at home or in a residential or nursing home. → LONG-TERM CARE

> 2.4 million people are claiming Incapacity Benefit *

> 4 million people are living on Disability Living Allowance *

What questions will I be asked?
Questions can and do vary. You must make known any diagnosis, treatment or tests for major illnesses, including cancer, heart problems, diabetes and multiple sclerosis. You must also reveal any medication you receive and say if you've been refused cover elsewhere.

Weight and height must be declared. Insurers then use this information to calculate your body mass index – an indication of your health. You may need to disclose HIV tests and hazardous pursuits.

Will I have to undergo a medical?
Fewer than five per cent of applicants are asked to take a medical. Tests normally apply to higher risks or people wanting large sums insured.   ▶

Why do insurers turn claims down?

If you don't give relevant medical information or if you bend the truth about your lifestyle habits and the insurer finds out, they could refuse a payout when you really need the financial support. If in doubt, disclose everything and give the insurer access to your medical records.

If you've failed to disclose some vital information, the insurance company may reject your claim application. If for example you've taken a policy out as a non-smoker, but later file a claim for lung cancer, the insurer can investigate using a cotinine test, which involves a swab from your mouth. Similarly, random blood and liver checks may be requested. Up to 25 or 30 units of alcohol a week (15 pints of beer or 4 bottles of wine) may not affect the premium, but this depends on your build.

> Nearly 2 million people of working age will be off work for at least six months at any time through sickness or disability *

* Source: National Statistics Online (2003)

Are premiums affected by other factors?

Insurers for PMI could determine the price of premiums based upon the area you live in and regional health issues. Although premiums are usually the same for Long-Term Care policies, the cost of local care can vary widely. Those in a more affluent area may need more cover, which in turn increases premiums.

Probabilities of suffering specific critical illness before age 65

	Heart Attack		Stroke		Cancer	
AGE	MALE	FEMALE	MALE	FEMALE	MALE	FEMALE
20–40	6%	2%	3%	2%	9%	11%
45	6%	2%	3%	2%	8%	10%
50	5%	2%	3%	2%	8%	9%
55	4%	1%	2%	1%	7%	7%
60	3%	1%	1%	1%	5%	4%

Source: Munich Re 24.07.02
Figures are based on a person currently being in good health.

I

IFA (Independent Financial Adviser).
➜ *Feature*

IMF (International Monetary Fund) –
Its main role is to lend money to
governments with serious economic
problems by issuing loans of mind-
boggling amounts.

IMPULSE SPENDING – one of the main
contributors to personal debt, when
you spot something you probably
don't need but can't resist.

INCOME – is seldom as
much as you believe you're
really worth. And you probably
have to pay tax on it too.

INCOME DRAWDOWN – an
arrangement to draw an income from
your pension, while leaving the rest
invested. ➜ ANNUITY

INCOME REPLACEMENT INSURANCE
– Who'll foot the bills if you are unable to
work? This cover typically provides 50 per
cent to 65 per cent of your regular
income continuing either until you return
to work, or reach your normal retirement
age, or you die. ➜ HEALTH INSURANCE

INCOME TAX – This tax on a person's
income is surprisingly still a 'temporary'
tax (since 1799) which expires on April
5th each year, and Parliament has to
renew it by an annual Finance Act. Speak
to your IFA for 'legal' ways to minimise
your bill. ➜ TAX TIPS

> **"The hardest thing in the world to
> understand"**
> *Albert Einstein*

INDEMNITY – an insurance policy
purchased to protect the lender against
loss, or if you default or cease to repay
the mortgage or other loan.

INDEX – like the FTSE 100 Share Index –
is a way of expressing the relative values
of a group of stocks and shares. The
values are weighted and enable anyone
who's interested to gain an indication of
how various sectors of the economy are
performing.

IFA

Do you need one?

Even the most clued-up investor can be bamboozled by the sheer choice and constant changes in the financial world. Using an IFA (Independent Financial Adviser) gives you access to thousands of options without the headache.

Ranging from individuals to larger firms, qualified IFAs will question and research your financial goals before making any recommendations.
As well as tackling specific issues, IFAs will usually look at your whole financial situation, presenting options that will make your money work harder.

Finding an IFA

- **Ask friends or family to recommend an IFA as a starting point.**

- **Organisations can put you in touch with IFAs in your area.** → CONTACTS

- **Speak to a few IFAs to find one who you feel understands you and your needs.**

- **Are they what they say they are?**

- **How long have they been trading as an IFA?**

- **Are they part of a larger network?**

- **Do they have references from other clients?**

- **Is there an area that they specialise in?**

- **How quickly will they respond to your financial requests?**

Are IFAs qualified?

An IFA must have passed the Financial Planning Certificates 1,2 and 3, or equivalent. Many argue that these are only basic exams and ideally IFAs should also have gained the Advanced Financial Planning Certificate, but this isn't a requirement. If IFAs are advising on either pension opt outs or occupational transfer schemes, they must be authorised pension transfer specialists.

Check with the Financial Services Authority (FSA) that your IFA is registered and what services they're authorised to offer.

From 31 October 2004, mortgage advisers will have to be authorised by the FSA, and by 15 January 2005 all general insurance and term assurance advisers need to be authorised.

Working with your IFA

During your first conversation, an IFA needs to make clear that at this stage he or she can only give non-specific advice. They must also be authorised (registered by the FSA) to give advice on investment products such as pensions, life assurance, investments and unit trusts and are legally bound to do the following:
• Confirm that they are independent (even though, by definition, they are).
• Get to know your requirements as a client. Most complete a 'fact find' questionnaire on your finances, exploring

your financial and personal circumstances. Be truthful, or the end advice may be unsuitable.

• Explain clearly why products they've selected are suitable for you, putting this in writing.

• Give you a key features document clarifying how much you're investing and into what funds, and highlighting the level of risk, aims and benefits of the product.

• Explain the cooling off period.

• Payments should be made directly to the product provider.

How do IFAs charge?

IFAs can work for either a fee or receive commission from providers.

Fees – Fees are based on the advice given, rather than any products arranged – either a set amount or hourly rate. The fees can be offset against commission received by the IFA, which can lessen the cost for you. But note that VAT may be payable on fees. Payment is normally made once the advice is finalised.

Commission – Commission is paid to the IFA by the product provider, out of charges. The commission must be disclosed to you before completing an application form.

Other advisers

In the future there will be three types of financial adviser:

Tied advisers – only able to advise about products from one company

Multi-tied advisers – working for a bank or financial institution with links to a number of product providers (a likely future development)

Independent Financial Advisers – giving advice on products across the market

Solicitors – can give independent financial advice if authorised, but if they're certified by the Law Society, the scope of advice may be limited.

Accountants – many chartered accountants can offer advice, especially on areas such as tax. Like solicitors, their ability to give financial advice may be restricted.

Insurance

What is it?
Insurance is paying regular sums (premiums) to an insurer, who in turn agrees to pay money in the event of loss, damage, injury or death, depending on the nature of the contract. Virtually every conceivable risk or mishap is insurable.

How many types are there?
Main domestic categories include:
- Life
- Health
- Motor
- Home building and contents
- Travel
- Extended warranties
- Legal expenses and liability
- Pet

Some you really ought to have, others may not apply or can be skipped. The point is to protect yourself or those you care about from financial loss. There are crossovers between policies. Look at your home and motor insurance policies to see if basic liability and legal expenses cover is provided. Don't duplicate the cover.

Is insurance a legal requirement?
UK law requires any driver to have the minimum 'third party' motor insurance. For individuals, all other insurance is optional.

Must I have home insurance?
Whilst it's not a legal requirement, mortgage lenders normally insist on some basic home insurance coverage. It is sensible to protect your home against financial loss.

What about life cover?
It's advisable if you have a mortgage or people depending on you financially. Needs vary widely, but even with no dependants, some form of life protection is prudent.

Can I reduce premiums?
On motor policies, safe drivers are rewarded with No Claims Bonuses. After six years without claiming, you could be eligible for up to 65 per cent discount. Protecting cars and homes against break-ins can help you negotiate cost savings. Also, the higher your excess the lower your premiums. You can trim the cost of Permanent Health Insurance by agreeing a longer waiting period before your benefits start.

What does excess mean?
This is the portion of your loss that you pay before the insurance payments kick in. If your excess is £100, and a claim is £500, you pay the £100 and then the insurer will pay the remaining £400.

What else should I be aware of?
Premiums do vary considerably, based upon the risks and the quality of cover. If you are shopping around, make it known you are comparing the protection you'll get for the premiums being quoted. Your IFA will do this as a matter of course.

Interest Rates

All interest rates stem from the 'base rate' set by the Bank of England Monetary Policy Committee. Interest rates can work in your favour or against you.

Rising rates – good news or bad?
When rates are low it's not a good time to be living off savings. So a 0.25 per cent increase is good news for savers, who with £100,000 would pocket an extra £250 a year in interest. But the same increase applied to a repayment mortgage of £100,000 over 25 years would cost you £912 a year, which means an extra £76 a month.

Two things – risk and timescale – generally influence the rates set by financial providers. If you have cash to invest, an IFA will ask you how much risk you are prepared to take and how quickly you want to lay your hands on your cash.

In November 2003, base rate was 3.5 per cent, the lowest level since January 1955

If you want instant access through a deposit account, you can expect a poorer return than if you are prepared to lock in for a longer period. The same applies to borrowing money. Mortgages for 25 years charge a relatively low rate of interest compared to short-term loans.

Caution – low rates are tempting for borrowers but if interest rates double, your debt could soar. Don't overstretch and leave yourself exposed.

Borrowing money

Check the small print
Headline rates are not everything. APR is a warning of what it will cost you for the full term.

Annual Percentage Rate (APR)
When looking at mortgages and loans, the quoted rate is the percentage for repaying the loan. The APR calculates the total amount of interest you will pay over the loan, including any charges, and breaks it down into an annual rate. It's a useful way to discover what you'll really be paying for credit.

In the past 30 years, Bank of England base rate has varied between a high of 17 per cent in November 1979 and a low of 3.5 per cent in July 2003.

If the APR is a lot higher than the quoted rate, this may indicate higher closing costs. This means the APR is a true value of the loan if you stay with the provider for the long-term and a good indication of how competitive it is against other lenders in the market.

Beware low introductory rates

To attract your attention, mortgage and other lenders (and credit cards) advertise a 'headline rate' to reel you in. This is a short-term interest rate, maybe for six months, possibly a couple of years – and after this period you'll normally revert to the lender's standard rate.

It can be a useful way to save money, if you can move your loan once the special rate has ended. 'Rate tarts', jump from one attractive interest rate offer to another. These special offers are great if you are able to come out of the loan when the special rate ends, but could cost dearly if you are tied in with a high APR.

The facts on flat rates

Not as common nowadays, but typically used to finance buying a car, flat interest rates shouldn't be mixed up with fixed rates. For example, a 7 per cent flat rate means you'll be paying 7 per cent of the initial loan every month for the full term of the loan. Read the small print and you'll probably discover the APR is nearer 21 per cent. By comparison, a fixed rate of 7 per cent is what you'll pay in interest for a set period of time. They sound similar offers, but will have very different impacts on your purse.

Saving money

Annual Equivalent Rate (AER)

Put simply, this shows you the return you could expect over a year on a savings or investment account, and is the percentage of interest rolled up and paid annually. AERs must now be published in all advertisements, letting you compare investments that run for different lengths of time.

Like APRs, the quoted rates and AER can vary. For example, a gross rate on an investment bond may be quoted as 5 per cent per annum, while the AER is given as 4.5 per cent, because the bond includes a six-month bonus of 1 per cent. After the first six months, the interest is 4 per cent, meaning the AER is actually 4.5 per cent.

Buying your annuity

When interest rates are low – as they have been in recent years – your retirement income from annuities can be severely dented. Timing is everything when buying your annuity. If you can afford to, it may be better to put off setting up your annuity until rates pick up.
➔ ANNUITY

Your IFA can help you to take advantage of interest rate structures – reducing short-term borrowings and increasing long-term investments.

> The all-time high for mortgages was in 1979, when base rate reached 17 per cent

INDEX-LINKED – something that rises (or falls) automatically in line with a defined index, typically the retail prices index as this reflects changes in the cost of living.

INFLATION – typically reduces spending power, as the cost of goods rise.

INHERITANCE TAX – the tax payable after death based upon the value of your assets over the set threshold (£255,000 at present). Anything above that amount is taxed at 40 per cent, but no tax is payable if the beneficiary is a surviving spouse.
➔ WILLS

INLAND REVENUE – responsible for the collection of all taxes (with the exception of VAT). People who complain about what the Revenue does can be divided into two groups – men and women.

INSIDER – a person privy to confidential information, which could be used to gain some financial advantage in the market. Insider trading is highly illegal.

INTELLIGENCE – the thing we keep searching for in outer space, which suggests there's not much here.

INTEREST – money paid for the use of money borrowed. ➔ INTEREST RATES

INTERIM DIVIDEND – a dividend payment to shareholders made during the course of the financial year, rather than at the end. Most public companies in the UK make an interim dividend payment after the half-year results.

INTERMEDIARY – a financial middleman. See *Broker*.

INTUITION – often used as the basis for making an investment decision, and especially for justifying decisions that turned out badly.

INVESTMENT CLUB – a group of people who share a common interest to invest in the stock market. There are more than 10,000 clubs in the UK.
➔ STOCKS AND SHARES

INVESTMENT MANAGEMENT ASSOCIATION (IMA) – the UK trade body for the professional investment management industry.

INVESTMENT TRUST – a fund set up as a quoted company on the stock exchange, which buys and sells shares in other companies.

ISA (Individual Savings Account) – a tax-efficient savings plan, which can hold cash, stocks and shares, and life assurance. ➔ SAVINGS

Investments

An IFA can help tailor your investments based upon your immediate and long-term objectives, personal attitude to risk, financial position, current investments, and performance prospects. There are many investment choices, posing different degrees of risk and offering different returns. The key is to know what you are buying, and why. The final decision is yours and yours alone.

- Are you looking for income or growth?
- Are you looking for a short-term or long-term return?
- What fees will you be paying?
- How has it performed in the past? Does it have a good track record?
- Is it in a sector you think will do well? What are your reasons for thinking this?
- Is this fund offering something unique? How does it differ from the competitors?
- Where do the fund managers rank in the league tables published in investor magazines?

Before you decide, see our 'Richter Scale' of investment risk. ▶

Bare Essentials

- **Investments have no guarantees. Sector, market, inflation, currency and political changes can all impact on the performance of your fund.**

- **Choosing the right vehicle for your current investment need is vital.**

- **Know what you are buying. There are thousands of investment variations, to suit particular types of investor or objectives.**

- **Do your homework before setting off.**

- **For some safety in numbers for beginners, opt for unit trusts or OEICs – Open Ended Investment Companies – and pool your investment. Alternatively, join an investment club to pick up some ideas.** *See Investment Club.*

Risk means different things to different people, but ultimately it is the possibility you could lose your money. Investors should never underestimate the risk factor.

Some people brave high risks, others take a belt and braces approach. Neither is right nor wrong – it simply depends on your short and long-term investment goals and how much you can afford to lose.

Gilts

(UK Government bonds) – Gilts, or gilt-edged securities, are UK Government bonds or securities issued to raise public funds. Because they are Government-backed they are very safe and secure, hence 'gilt-edged'. The stocks are mostly fixed-interest but some are index-linked.

Pooled Investments

(Invested in bonds) Money is collected together from thousands of individual investors, and used to buy a portfolio of bonds. This portfolio is divided into individual units, which can be bought and sold by investors. Unit trusts invested in bonds reduce the degree of specific risk even further.

Corporate Bonds

Issued by companies to raise funds, these are less secure than Government bonds. Large stable companies are almost as safe as gilts, but bonds issued by small new firms may be quite risky. Blue Chip firms pay relatively low interest rates, whereas 'junk bonds' – the higher risk – tend to deliver higher rates.

Unit Trusts

(Invested in shares) A variety of unit trust funds invest in shares. Index tracker funds follow the stock market index (FTSE). Equity income funds concentrate on companies that pay high dividends, and are ideal for people looking for income. The choice is wide, so speak to an IFA.

LOW RISK

The 'Richter Scale' of investment risk

Large Cap Shares

(Blue Chip companies) These shares in the large, well-established UK companies make up the FTSE 100. They generally have a track record for increasing profits so can be less risky. Even though they are less likely to rise and fall significantly in value, major changes do claim casualties.

Mid Caps

(Shares) These are large companies just outside the FTSE 100, referred to as Mid Cap companies. These can be slightly riskier than Blue Chip companies as share prices tend to move by larger amounts. However, this can be a strong growth area for investors if you can afford the risk.

Small Caps

(Shares) These smaller shares on the stock market and the Alternative Investment Market contain more newcomers and are generally the most risky share investment. If you pick a good one, the financial rewards can be good. But prepare yourself for rapid swings in value.

Futures

(Including options, derivatives, real estate investment trusts) This is real gambling. Futures are much more speculative, as effectively you are betting on what is going to happen in the future. Not one for the wary investor.

HIGH RISK

WEALTH WARNING
IF AN INVESTMENT LOOKS TOO GOOD TO BE TRUE, IT USUALLY IS

Investing – still a risky business?

The State is shifting more and more responsibility onto individuals, so consumers are having to make important financial decisions from very early in life. To minimise the risks, Paul Wright of Zurich believes that professional advice is increasingly important.

People are realising they need to provide for and protect themselves throughout life – from paying for education, the first mortgage and income protection, through to pensions and annuities.

It can be argued that investment is all about managing risk. Without doubt, understanding risk and, more importantly, how you perceive and feel about risk is crucial to making a sound investment decision. While consumers have more access to information than ever before, which is undoubtedly a good thing, it doesn't mean they're able to pinpoint the most suitable investment portfolio for themselves.

With a myriad of products on the market, it can be a daunting process finding the best investment. Advisers shoulder a great responsibility – to know their customer and, before recommending a suitable product, thoroughly testing their client's attitudes to the potential ups and downs. Investors don't always fully appreciate the relationship between risk and reward, volatility or their own attitude to risk. As a result, their expectations of performance (particularly in the short term) may well be unrealistic, and therefore not met.

Reducing the risk

In the current climate, many investors are seeking to maximise returns with minimal risk – not an easy objective in an environment of low interest rates, low inflation and, arguably, still volatile stock markets. This pattern was reinforced by research commissioned by Zurich and undertaken by The Henley Centre, exploring consumer attitudes to risk. Two messages came out loud and clear. The first was that when people are making investment decisions they need to consider carefully their own attitudes to risk – and to do this properly, they need information. The second was that, as investors, we're all getting more cautious about our investment decisions.

The lesson for providers and advisers alike is clear – we all need to adjust to changing customer needs in these more cautious times.

> As investors, we're all getting more cautious about our investment decisions

As an industry, we need to give our customers the products they want, and quality advice to make sure they are the right products. It's encouraging that companies are recognising this and we're beginning to see a new generation of products that offer transparency and security for the customer despite volatile markets. Zurich-owned Sterling, as a result of the Henley Centre Research, has redesigned its investment proposition, transforming customer needs into tangible products. The launch last year of Sterling's Protected Profits Fund and the recent launch of new, risk-rated, multi-manager fund of fund portfolios mark this evolution of products and services targeted towards today's investor.

Risk awareness and advice

Just as the industry needs to react to these changing circumstances, so too does the consumer. Great efforts are being made by a number of organisations to instil an understanding of financial services from a young age, including the Personal Finance Education Group under the chairmanship of Ron Sandler. The ABI's Raising Standards Scheme is also working hard to give consumers clear information and processes. Individuals need to take advantage of these developments – it's a two-way process that works on the basis of a partnership approach. A financially astute, well-guided investor who understands their attitude towards risk and reward is the ultimate aim.

Advisers are crucial to this evolution. Greater education through more information is important. But that's not the same as an investor recognising his or her risk threshold and understanding the context of the investment decisions needed. That's where your adviser can step in to help.

ZURICH

J

JACKPOT – One day we may win it. Until then …

JARGON – the art of making things sound more complicated than they really are. How are we doing so far?

JOBSEEKERS' ALLOWANCE – a benefit paid to an unemployed person for a period of up to six months, provided the claimant is capable of working, available for work and actively seeking work. The amount varies with age.

JOINT LIABILITY – usually a borrowing/lending arrangement where joint liability gives the lender more avenues of redress in the case of default. It may also apply to credit card purchases where the card issuer and the supplier of the goods are equally responsible for all purchases above £100.

JOINT OWNERSHIP – the owning of a property by more than one person. Not restricted to married couples, it's now becoming common for friends to club together and jointly buy a property that they could not afford individually.

JUNGLE – a place of bewildering confusion and dangerous animals, and so nothing like the financial jungle. Your IFA is at hand to guide you through it.

JUNIOR MARKET – another name for the Alternative Investment Market, where smaller companies take their first steps on the stock market. See *AIM*.

JUNK BONDS – see *High Yield Bonds* and *Corporate Bonds*.

K

KICKBACK – an illegal or unethical payment or commission that is made to someone for assisting a business deal.

KIDS – your greatest asset and liability all rolled into one, or however many you may have. Prepare yourself for the financial onslaught. → CHILDREN

KIN (NEXT OF) – In fact, there is no statutory definition for this term, but it is generally taken to mean the nearest relative by marriage, blood, or adoption. It is often required in a medical context or when applying for life insurance.

KNOWLEDGE – Those with knowledge say that a little knowledge is a dangerous thing, which may be good enough reason to consult an IFA. But then, they also say that ignorance is bliss.

Killer questions to ask your IFA

- **How will you get paid for giving me advice?**

- **Is it better to pay you a fee, or do I benefit more if you get commission?**

- **Which product areas do you specialise in?**

- **How many providers do you look at before making a recommendation?**

- **How will the charges affect the returns I get on my policy?**

- **What are the pros and cons of each suggested product?**

- **What risks are involved?**

- **What am I committing myself to?**

- **What are the problems if I change my mind or need the money earlier than anticipated?**

- **Could I lose my money?**

L

LANDLADY – the butt of much politically incorrect humour, and the female equivalent of Landlord.

LANDLORD – someone who owns land or property that is rented to a paying tenant. Or more refreshingly, a man who runs a pub.

LAW SOCIETY – the professional body that controls all practising solicitors, who may be able to help if you have an issue with your solicitor that cannot be resolved.

LAWYER – any highly-trained and well-paid member of the legal profession who can act on behalf of clients in legal matters, and also put up with insulting jokes: "How can you tell when lawyers are lying? … Their lips move."

LEASE – a written contract between two parties for letting a building, a piece of land, plant, machinery or equipment for an agreed period of time and at an agreed price or rent.

LEASEHOLD – a type of ownership of property, where the property is held on a lease for a fixed period of time.

LEGAL EXPENSES INSURANCE – insurance that provides financial aid if you go to court. Legal Aid is restricted to a small number of people, and many insurers now provide Legal Expenses Insurance as an add-on benefit to home and motor policies. Some will charge a minimal fee, while others include it as part of the comprehensive insurance package. Check the details of your policies.

LIABILITY – anything (or anyone) that could be your responsibility to pay for, sooner or later.

LIABILITY INSURANCE – financial protection for companies and individuals against accidents and mishaps for which they may be held legally responsible. For companies there are two types: Employers' Liability covers claims from employees, and Public Liability covers claims from the general public. For individuals, a whole range of personal liability insurances can be tailored to particular needs, such as sporting activities, travel, occupation or house ownership.

LIBOR (London Inter Bank Offer Rate) – the rate of interest that banks will offer to lend money to one another in the 'wholesale' money markets of London. It doesn't really affect individual borrowers unless you have a mortgage linked to LIBOR.

LIFE INSURANCE – because you're worth it. ➔ *Feature*

Life Insurance

How much do you need?

There is no 'one size fits all'. The key is to consider your current salary and the level of income that your dependants would need in order to maintain their standard of living. The normal rule of thumb is to multiply your salary by ten in order to calculate the amount of cover. But, as ever, it depends on your circumstances so you should speak to an IFA.

If you have a mortgage, you must have enough insurance to cover the balance outstanding. Next, look at your life. Who depends on you to 'bring home the bacon'? If suddenly you're not there tomorrow, how much will they need?

Parents should quantify their children's financial needs. It depends on age – with younger children allow for the cost of day-care, schooling and university. If your partner has a good income, he or she may not need as much as a partner with no income of their own.

If you're married, there are no guarantees that your partner will meet someone else to share the load if you die. Anyone with family and financial obligations shouldn't think "do I need protection?", but rather "what kind and how much?".

An IFA will be able to tailor cover to meet your individual circumstances. ▶

What choice is there?

The two key areas are term assurance and whole of life.

Term assurance is the most common. It's competitively priced, with cover for a set term of years and no payout if you live to the end:

- **Level Term** – in most cases, premiums that don't change during the policy.
- **Escalating Term** – lower sums assured when younger, which rise over time. So too do the premiums.
- **Decreasing Term** – premiums stay the same, but cover reduces during the term, dropping off steeply at the end of the term. Typically this is used with repayment mortgages.
- **Convertible Term** – giving the option to convert a policy into a whole-of-life policy.

Whole-of-life insurance pays cash benefits regardless of when you die. There are advantages to this cover – mainly that you have continuous cover and the ability to cash it in. But if you live until 95, consider whether your spouse or children will really need, say, £200,000?

Bare Essentials

- Buy what you need to meet your family's needs.

- Don't undervalue your life and the financial contribution you make.

- Do the maths and ask your IFA about options.

DANGER – Risk of death

Probabilities of dying before age 65*

AGE	MALE	FEMALE
20–40	15%	9%
40	14%	9%
45	13%	8%
50	12%	8%
55	10%	6%
60	7%	4%

*Based on a person currently in good health
Source: Munich Re

Are lump sums the only option?

Family Income Benefit insurance pays an income each year – possibly equivalent to your current salary.

Can I insure anyone's life?

You can only insure people who are providing for you. The Life Assurance Act of 1774 introduced the concept of insurable interest after a spate of incidents where gamblers insured others' lives who later met a sticky end.

For people who rely on financial contributions, if you can quantify the loss, you can insure their life for that sum and no more. For example:

- Your life and your spouse's life
- Ex-spouse's maintenance payments
- Children financing parental long-term care
- Business partners providing specialist skills
- Key employees and their contribution to profits.

LIMITED COMPANY – a registered company in which the shareholders' liability for the company's debts is limited to the face value of the shares they hold. The shares of a Private Limited Company (abbreviated to Ltd) cannot be traded on the Stock Exchange, those of a Public Limited Company (abbreviated to Plc) can, so long as they are listed.

LISTED COMPANY – a company whose shares are quoted on the main market of the London Stock Exchange. To reach the ranks of a listed company, your financial well being will be scrutinised and the Quotations Committee of the Stock Exchange must accept your shares.

LLOYD'S OF LONDON – still regarded as one of the most powerful players in the insurance industry. While Lloyd's associated companies provide life assurance and general insurance, Lloyd's is better known as a global marine and aviation insurer.

LOAN – money lent to a borrower that is repaid with interest.

LOAN SHARK – a lender who provides money when nobody else will, at extortionate rates of interest, and who has persuasive ways of ensuring repayment. To be avoided. If you have debt problems, talk to the Consumer Credit Counselling Service or National Debtline. → CONTACTS

LOAN TO VALUE – the relationship between the amount of a mortgage and the value of the property, expressed as a percentage. For example, if a house is valued at £100,000 and you want a mortgage of £85,000, the Loan to Value is 85 per cent. Banks and Building Societies will state a maximum LTV they permit for any loan. When the LTV is high, they may also charge a higher interest rate, because they regard their risk as higher.

LONG-TERM CARE INSURANCE – a fairly recent addition to the UK insurance market, providing financial assistance for care either at home or in a residential nursing home. Cover can be arranged for a fixed number of years or indefinitely, and premiums are usually paid monthly. → LONG-TERM CARE

LOSS ADJUSTER – a qualified specialist who assesses an insurance claim.

Low mortgage rate for life

Could there be a genuinely new approach to making mortgages simple to understand and rewarding to keep? Abbey believes there is, and explains how they're offering a guaranteed discount for the entire life of a mortgage, in return for an upfront fee.

Finding a way to reward existing customers, whilst at the same time making upfront deals attractive to new customers, has challenged mortgage lenders for years. None of the solutions has really worked, often just causing problems.

As one contribution to try to make life easier, Abbey is offering a guaranteed discount for the entire life of a mortgage, in return for an upfront fee. This makes the prospect of longer term mortgages much more attractive. There are no penalties for early repayment or other hidden charges. The low rate, which is a discount on Abbey's Flexible Plus mortgage, is available to both new and existing customers. The move is part of our latest efforts to make it simpler and easier to choose the right mortgage, which also includes new 'pick-'n'-mix' options. In addition, it's a first step towards delivering on our promise to reward loyal mortgage customers in a fair and consistent way.

Life-time guaranteed discount

By paying an upfront fee of £1,000, customers will pay just 0.50 per cent above the Bank of England base rate, which is guaranteed for the life of the mortgage. So for example, if the base rate is 4.25 per cent, Abbey's discounted rate will be 4.75 per cent, which means a customer could save many thousands of pounds over the life of their mortgage.

Customers will be able to tailor their basic choice of mortgage with add-ons from a 'pick-'n'-mix' list, building a mortgage that really meets their needs. The options are clearly priced so customers can see exactly what they're paying for and what impact it has on their mortgage interest rate – either increasing or decreasing it.

Straightforward Steps

Step 1: Intermediary recommends the mortgage most appropriate to the customer's needs from the Abbey range.

Step 2: The amount of the deposit determines the initial mortgage interest rate the customer will pay.

Step 3: Intermediary and customer discuss and agree any additional options from the 'pick-'n'-mix' list.

Pick-'n'-mix

Among the options that can be added are:

■ 'Guaranteed deal for life' – pay an upfront fee of £1,000 to guarantee the mortgage rate will remain 0.50 per cent above the Bank of England base rate for the life of the mortgage.

■ 'Help with fees' – Abbey pays for a valuation and provides £250 cashback.

■ 'Pay now and save ' – Customers can pay an upfront fee to obtain an even lower mortgage interest rate during the special offer period.

With the introduction of clearly priced 'add-ons' for mortgages, intermediaries will be able to advise and help their clients create the best possible mortgage for their needs. There's still a lot of work to do, but we are committed to improving things for financial advisers and our customers.

Long-term Care

As you get older, you might develop health problems that could make it difficult to cope with everyday tasks. So you might need help to stay in your own home or move into a care home. The State may provide some help towards the cost of this care depending on your personal circumstances.

How do you pay for long-term care?

If you need long-term care you should check with your local authority about the support they give. The social services department will make an assessment of your care needs. The amount of free long-term care support you receive will depend on your income and savings, and whereabouts in the British Isles you live. The rules can differ in England, Scotland and Wales.

If you don't qualify for financial help under the local authority assessment, you will normally be expected to pay for care out of your own income (probably your pension) and, if your capital is high enough, out of your savings as well. Alternatively, you can consider releasing money from the value of your home or purchasing long-term care insurance to offset some or all of the cost of your care needs.

How much does long-term care insurance cost?

This depends on your age, gender and medical history. Women pay more than men because they tend to live longer. The average benefit bought is about £800 a month or £10,000 a year. For a 65-year-old woman, this would cost around £13,000 as a lump sum or £70 a month, which would rise with inflation. A man would pay £7,000 or £55 per month.

What is the likelihood of needing this care?

One in four people over 85 ends up in a nursing or residential care home. The costs can range from £20,000 to £40,000 a year.

The best advice is to seek professional advice as to all the options available to you. Speak to your IFA.

M

MARKET CAPITALISATION – the total value of a company, measured by the value of stock market shares multiplied by the number of shares in circulation.

MARRIAGE – see *Liability*.

MATTRESS – not the place to keep your surplus cash. Speak to your IFA.

MAXI ISA → SAVINGS

MEANS TESTING – a method to measure and dispense state benefits to people who are unemployed or on a low income. The Working Tax Credit is one example. If you apply, your financial 'means' will be examined to make certain you qualify for help.

MICROPAL RATINGS – an independent fund analyst that monitors and rates fund performance.

MINI ISA → SAVINGS

Who wants to be a millionaire?

- More than half of all liquid wealth in the UK – £542 billion out of a total of £1,071 trillion, not counting homes, second homes, pensions and insurance but including investment property – is owned by millionaires. Less than 1 per cent is owned by the least well-off 50 per cent of the adult population.

- Of the UK's 135,000 millionaires, 104,000 are men and 31,000 are women – but the proportion of women is growing year by year.

- The average age of millionaires is late fifties, and over a third are retired or semi-retired. It takes time to accumulate wealth.

- The average millionaire has £4.2 million in liquid assets, and over a further £1 million in homes and pensions – but the average is skewed by the immense wealth of the richest multi-millionaires.

- More than half of all millionaires own or owned their own businesses or were partners in professional practices. Ownership is the single best route to wealth.

- Millionaires hold a third of their liquid wealth in company shares, and about 10 per cent in each of Unit Trusts/OEICS, bonds and cash. Residential and commercial investment property is the biggest single holding after company shares.

Source: Tulip Financial Research Limited, 2004.
www.tulipresearch.com

Mortgages

There is a wide choice of mortgages, and feeling confident in your choice is vital.

Offset mortgages

These are fairly new in the market and link to your savings and bank account. You are only charged interest on the mortgage amount left when they subtract the total of these balances from your mortgage. You won't earn interest on savings – a pitfall for low-rate tax payers, but a plus for higher-rate payers, who'll be taxed on any savings interest anyway.

Flexible mortgages

These allow you to pay your mortgage off early with no penalty, or take a payment holiday when financial difficulties arise. Disciplined savers now use this as part of their long-term investment plan, paying large amounts off that they can draw later to fund things like school fees.

Remortgaging

Why are people put off switching? Don't think that moving your mortgage means hiring the removal men and moving house. You can stay put, simply switch to another lender. With so many special

Repaying your mortgage

You'll pay your mortgage in monthly instalments, but first you'll need to decide between two options, 'repayment' and 'interest only'.

	How it works	Plus points	Pitfalls
Repayment	You pay some interest and some capital each month, and the capital reduces over time.	There are no surprises. At the end of the term, provided you've kept up with payments, you're guaranteed to pay off your mortgage.	Your monthly payment will generally be higher than interest only. There's no potential investment windfall at the end.
Interest only	All you pay each month is the interest on the amount borrowed. At the end of the term you will need enough funds to pay back the amount borrowed. Many choose an Individual Savings Account (ISA) to cover this lump sum.	Your investments may perform well, giving you surplus cash after paying off the mortgage. ISAs also benefit from tax advantages.	As endowment policyholders have discovered, you're relying on your chosen investments to perform well. If they don't, you could end up with a shortfall. It's up to you to monitor performance and check whether there is going to be enough to pay off the capital amount at the end.

incentives and deals, remortgaging could save you a lot of money.

Many thousands of homeowners remain with lenders on standard variable rates, when in fact they could have a better deal with a cheaper interest rate.

Because the industry is so competitive, the process can be quick and reasonably ▶

Interest Rate Options

You can choose how you want to be charged interest. You'll need to consider not only current interest rates, but also the likelihood of them rising or falling in the near future. The options are:

	How it works	Plus points	Pitfalls
Standard Variable rate	Rates tend to move up and down in line with the base rate set by the Bank of England.	Your payment will decrease if interest rates go down.	If interest rates rise, your payments are likely to increase in line with the base rate. The rate is variable and set by the lender.
Fixed rate	Your interest is guaranteed not to change for an agreed period of time, typically one to ten years.	You can be certain during that time your monthly payments won't change.	If interest rates fall below your fixed rate, you won't benefit. You may have to pay an Arrangement Fee or Early Redemption Penalties.
Capped rate	A fixed ceiling rate, so if interest rates rise, yours will not increase above this ceiling level.	You get a certain degree of protection if rates rise, and if they fall you will pay less.	The interest rate set for capped deals is often slightly higher than fixed rates. You may have to pay an Arrangement Fee or Early Redemption Penalties.
Discounted rate	You receive a discount on the variable rate for a set period.	Lower payments for the time of the discount.	You may have to pay an Arrangement Fee or Early Redemption Penalties.
Tracker rate	Rates are set at a certain margin above the Bank of England base rate and move in line with it.	If the base rate drops significantly, so will your payment. The rate is independent and not set by the lender.	Base rates can increase as well as drop. You'll need to check the signals from the markets. These tend to be more expensive than a fixed or discount rate in the early years.

stress free. Check with your current lender about redemption charges for moving. You may also have to pay an application fee, possibly even valuations and lawyer's fees, which can easily hit £800. New lenders sometimes pick up these charges. Ask your IFA to check out your options.

■ **The devil is in the detail. Check all the terms you're signing up to.**

■ **Get impartial advice.**

■ **Rates aren't everything. If it looks cheap, check to see if any strings are attached. You could be locked in for a set period.**

■ **Go independent for all the extras – you don't have to be tied to your mortgage lender for buildings and contents insurance and mortgage protection.**

■ **Mortgage providers generally lend 3–4 times a single income or 2–3 times a joint income.**

■ **If you've got a poor credit rating, seek out an IFA who can help find a lender who'll arrange a competitive mortgage.**

Cashbacks

Cashbacks are often used to attract first-time buyers. Although 5 per cent of £60,000 (£3,000) is useful for new homebuyers, you may forgo a better offer or be tied to a more expensive rate.

Protecting your mortgage

How would you and your family pay the mortgage if you were too ill to work or suddenly unemployed? Worse still, what if you died? A mortgage is one of the biggest financial commitments you're likely to make, so it's prudent to arrange some form of financial protection. The main options are:

Mortgage Payment Protection – Covering against the unexpected – an accident, a sudden illness or unemployment (through no fault of your own) – this insurance provides an income to cover your mortgage payments and property related insurance payments for up to twelve months.

Critical Illness Cover – This is paid as a tax-free lump sum to pay off your mortgage if you are diagnosed with a specific serious illness, such as cancer.

Life Insurance – An insurance plan that will repay your mortgage if you die during the term of the mortgage. You can opt for a decreasing term plan linked to the mortgage, which will repay whatever is owed during the mortgage term. There are many choices. Speak to your IFA.

➔ LIFE INSURANCE

MONETARY POLICY COMMITTEE –
The Bank of England's Monetary Policy
Committee decides the level of the base
rate each month. The Committee includes
the Bank of England Governor and two
Deputy Governors, plus six other
members (two from the Bank and four
experts from outside).

MONEY – apparently makes the world
go around, and yet the love of money is
the root of all evil. Also known as Dosh,
Dough, Readies, Wad, Lolly, Wedge,
Wonga, and Moolah – and that's just in
Del-Boy's dictionary.

Some money slang
£1 – Nicker, Quid, Squid
£5 – Fiver, Lady Godiva
£10 – Tenner, Pavarotti
£20 – Score
£25 – Pony
£50 – Bullseye
£100 – Ton
£500 – Monkey
£1000 – Grand
£2000 – Archer
£100,000 – Plum
£1,000,000 – Bernie

MONEY PURCHASE SCHEME – a
pension scheme into which a member
makes contributions. The final amount
will depend on the amount paid in and
the investment returns achieved.

MORTGAGES ➜ *Feature*

**MORTGAGE INDEMNITY
GUARANTEE** – insurance that covers the
lender should you default on your
mortgage at a time when your home is
worth less than the amount you have
borrowed (see *Negative Equity*). You pay,
but the insurance is to protect the lender,
not you. The lender can also pursue the
borrower for the balance outstanding.

MORTGAGE PAYMENT PROTECTION
– an insurance that pays your monthly
mortgage payments for a specified period
of time in the event that you cannot work
through sickness or accident or you are
made unemployed.

MOTOR INSURANCE ➜ INSURANCE

MUTUAL FUND – an open-ended fund
operated by an investment company.
Money is raised from investors and
invested in a group of assets in line with
the stated objectives.

MUTUAL SOCIETY – an organisation
owned by its members and run for their
benefit. See *Building Society* and *Friendly
Society*.

N

NASDAQ (The National Association of Securities Dealers Automated Quotations System) – an electronic stock market based in the USA, heavily biased towards small and new companies and all technology stocks.

NATIONAL DEBT – Governments often spend more in a year than they collect in tax revenues. The difference has to be borrowed, and becomes the National Debt. In boom times, some of this debt will be repaid. The UK National Debt stood at £434.5 billion at the end of 2002.

NATIONAL INSURANCE – a form of taxation rather than insurance that is paid by employees, employers and the self-employed. The amount paid is based on earnings. The contributions are used to fund, amongst other things, state pensions, unemployment benefits, sickness benefits, and the NHS.
➜ PENSIONS

NATIONAL SAVINGS – Government backed savings products, mostly aimed at the small investor. Through National Savings and Investments, the Treasury offers savings and many tax-free products that can be bought 'over post office counters'.

NEGATIVE EQUITY – when the amount outstanding on a mortgage is greater than the current value of the property.

NEST EGG – your pot of money reserved for rainy days, or to be enjoyed unconditionally when you retire. But it could crack if kept under the mattress.

NET INCOME – what you're left with after tax, National Insurance and any other deductions have been subtracted from your salary.

NO CLAIMS DISCOUNT – a reward usually linked to motor insurance, offering discounts to customers with a good claims history. ➜ INSURANCE

NOMINAL INTEREST RATE (NIR) – the rate of interest a lender will use to calculate the amount you actually owe them if you decide to clear a loan early. The NIR is usually slightly less than the APR. ➜ INTEREST RATES

NOMINATION FORM – see *Expression of Wish*.

NYSE (New York Stock Exchange) – the main stock market in the USA.

OBLIGATION – something that is written in stone. Failure to meet your payment obligations on a mortgage or other financial products will put you in default.

OCCUPATIONAL PENSION SCHEMES – also referred to as Company Pension Schemes, these are offered by employers for the benefit of their workforce. Arranged privately, they can vary widely.

There are usually two types – final salary and money purchase schemes.
→ PENSIONS

OCTOBER
"This is one of the particularly dangerous months to invest in stocks. Other dangerous months are July, January, September, April, November, May, March, June, December, August and February."
Mark Twain

OEIC (Open-Ended Investment Company) – a pooled investment similar to Unit Trusts, but OEICs issue shares instead of units. They normally quote a single price for buying and selling.

OFFICE OF FAIR TRADING (OFT) – a Government agency to protect consumers and their rights. Also keeps a watchful eye on businesses, making sure they compete and operate fairly.
→ CONTACTS

OFFSET – a method of calculating the balance owed. Where you owe an amount to someone, who in turn owes money to you, it's more efficient to cancel out the debt. Any difference between payments is referred to as an offset.

OFFSET MORTGAGE – This type of account links your current or savings account 'credit' balances to your mortgage. It gives more flexibility and can cut down on the amount of interest you pay. → MORTGAGES

OFFSHORE – funds or savings accounts held outside the United Kingdom, usually in so-called tax havens. Deciding to invest offshore depends on your circumstances, and you should always seek specialist advice.

OMBUDSMAN – a public servant who investigates and deals with complaints from individuals about their treatment by a range of businesses. The most relevant is the Financial Ombudsman Service.
→ CONTACTS

ONLINE – any communication made through the Internet.

> For online banking and payment security, always look for the padlock sign in the bottom bar of your browser. It means that the site you are visiting has automatically provided a recognised security certificate. You should also check that the address begins 'https'.
>
>

OPAS (the Pensions Advisory Service) – your port of call if you have a grievance about a personal pension or occupational pension scheme. It acts as a mediator between you and the scheme managers.
→ CONTACTS

OPEN-ENDED FUNDS – an investment fund where the number of units issued varies from day to day. Unit trusts are an example of open-ended funds, whereas investment trusts are closed-ended funds.

OPEN MARKET OPTION – your right as a consumer to buy your annuity from any provider including the one that administered your pension. → ANNUITY

ORDINARY SHARES – shares in a company, owned by people who are the legal owners of the company and entitled to receive dividends out of any profits, after the holders of preference shares have been paid. If the company goes bust, ordinary shareholders will lose their money.

OUTGOINGS – all the ways in which money is spent. Some outgoings are regular bills you'll have control over, others can occur without warning – which is why a nest egg can be handy. See *Nest Egg*.

OVERDRAFT – a 'short-term' arrangement with a bank to borrow money, to meet an unexpected requirement. Interest will be charged, and on the whole, an agreed overdraft is less costly than an unauthorised one.

P

PARENTS – If you live long enough, you may have the chance to get even with your children. They're legally your financial dependants until age 18, but you could become their liability eventually.

PAYE (Pay As You Earn) – the system by which your employer deducts income tax from your wages and pays the money to the Inland Revenue. But we're each liable as individuals for the tax on our total income. How honest are you?

PENALTIES – can be more painful than a kick. If you supply incorrect information to the Inland Revenue, or miss their time limit, you may be liable to pay a penalty as well as any tax due. Penalties may also be charged if you settle a fixed rate mortgage early, or some other kinds of loan. See *Early Redemption*.

PENSIONS – are never big enough.
➜ *Feature*

P/E RATIO – the Price/Earnings Ratio of a share. This is the price at which a share can be bought or sold, divided by the earnings per share (EPS). The experts compare P/E ratios of similar companies. A high P/E ratio may suggest the market expects that company's profits to grow rapidly, a low P/E ratio may suggest little or no growth.

PERCENTAGE – a standard way to show the proportion between two numbers, in particular the interest you'll earn or have to pay in relation to the capital.

Calculating percentages

If you deposit £1,000 in the bank and earn 2.5 per cent annual interest, you work out the money you'll earn in one year like this:

£1,000 times 2.5 divided by 100 = **£25.00**

Working out what one number is as a percentage of another is a little trickier. For example, to calculate 25 as a percentage of 80 follow these steps:

Divide 25 by 80 (=0.3125),
then multiply by 100 (=31.25)
Answer, 25 is **31.25 per cent** of 80

PERMANENT HEALTH INSURANCE –
➜ HEALTH INSURANCE and *Hospital Cash Plans*.

PHASED RETIREMENT – a facility to use small segments of your pension to buy an annuity, as and when you need the income. ➜ ANNUITY

PLAIN ENGLISH – In finance, it means nothing's hidden in the small print or wrapped up in mystifying jargon. You should be so lucky.

Pensions – planning for retirement

How much will you need?
Imagine you were going to retire next week, and work out the figures in today's terms.

• What are your outgoings likely to be?

• What will you spend less on – mortgage, children, health insurance?

• What will you spend more on – holidays, hobbies, Private Medical Insurance, entertainment?

• Then, deduct your likely state pension.

That's the income you'll need, in today's terms, to fund your lifestyle in retirement.

The basic state pension
Currently this is £77.45 a week or £123.80 for couples. To qualify for the full pension, you must pay or be credited with Class 1 or Class 2 contributions for 90 per cent of your working life. To find out what your projected state pension will be, complete a BR19 form available from your Social Security office or www.dwp.gov.uk

Your own pension pot
To give you an income of £20,000 a year today, assuming an annuity rate of 5 per cent, you'd need £400,000 in your pension pot.

If you're not due to retire for say 30 years, then you'll also need to allow for inflation as £20,000 won't have the same buying power as it does today. Generally the value of your income drops by one third every ten years if you assume 4 per cent inflation in real pay. So you'd need an annual income of £60,000 in 30 years, or a pension pot of £1.2 million based on today's annuity rates.

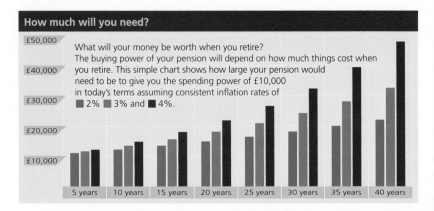

How much will you need?

What will your money be worth when you retire?
The buying power of your pension will depend on how much things cost when you retire. This simple chart shows how large your pension would need to be to give you the spending power of £10,000 in today's terms assuming consistent inflation rates of ■ 2% ■ 3% and ■ 4%.

What pension scheme is best for you?

Your IFA will advise you on the pension strategy that's best for you and your circumstances.

The Government is planning to make things simpler. Over the years, different regulations have been applied according to the type of pension and when it was taken out. The aim is to have one set of rules for all pensions. April 2005 is the target date, but there's no guarantee that the reforms will take place.

Should you invest all your savings in a pension scheme?

Generally no. Although there are considerable tax breaks, there are restrictions on when and how you can get money out. Consider balancing a pension with other investments and cash savings.

Tax relief on pension contributions

If you are in a Personal Pension or Stakeholder Plan, or have a Free Standing Additional Voluntary Contribution plan (FSAVC), every £1,000 contribution will cost you £780. The taxman chips in the rest. Higher-rate taxpayers can claim back an additional 18 per cent, giving you a £1,000 contribution for just £600.

Other arrangements apply to Retirement Annuity Contracts or any other Occupational Pension schemes. However, the level of tax relief individuals are entitled to is the same, no matter what kind of arrangement you have.

If I'm in an Occupational Pension scheme, can I take out a Personal Pension or Stakeholder Plan?

Yes, in certain circumstances. If you're not a controlling director you may be able to contribute up to £3,600 per annum.

What about charges?

Charges are important. Invest £10,000 in a plan with a 3 per cent charge and 7 per cent growth, and the fund will be worth £39,460 after 35 years. The same money in a Stakeholder Plan with a 1 per cent charge and 7 per cent growth would be worth £76,860.

Pensions – approaching retirement

What does my SMPI statement mean?

This is a Statutory Money Purchase Illustration from your pension provider showing the pension's current value, its projected value and the annual retirement income it may buy. It's an indication of what your pension may be worth at today's prices.

I've moved employers and have several pension schemes. How do I find out their total value?

You need to get a benefit statement from each scheme provider. For occupational pensions contact the HR department. It's vital to maintain contact with the scheme administrators, informing them of any address changes.

Should I transfer my Occupational Pension if I'm not confident in it?

You can request an estimate of the Transfer Value that will be available. It's essential to get some expert advice before deciding the best option.

How will I be paid my pension?

If you've a personal pension, you can normally take up to 25 per cent as a tax-free lump sum. The rest buys an annuity from an insurance company, who'll pay an annual income. With a final salary scheme you can also take a lump sum and a reduced annual pension, but the benefits are paid directly from the scheme.

I've been told my final salary pension is in deficit. Should I be worried?

While you may be concerned, employers have to continue to support the scheme. A deficit is just a snapshot of today's financial position – the situation may change. The big problem is when the deficit is large in relation to the assets of the employer.

If my company goes bust, do creditors have access to pension schemes?

No, a pension scheme is not a company asset. You can still invest in a personal pension scheme, but the employer won't make any more contributions. This is different for Occupational Pension schemes. If a member is no longer an employee of the company, he cannot contribute to the scheme. If scheme assets are not sufficient to cover liabilities, there'll be no employer to bail it out.

If I have a private pension, will I lose out on pension credit?

Small pensions will benefit from this credit. However, if your income is above a certain limit, you'll have no entitlement anyway.

Will I be covered by the Pension Protection Fund?

If you are in a final salary scheme, your employer will have to pay into the fund, and this will improve your security if the company is unable to fund the pension scheme. It is unlikely to start before 2005.

PLANNING – Good financial planning starts with where you are now, and where you want to be in the future. It would be worth speaking to an IFA.

POLICY – a document that sets out the terms and conditions of a contract, such as an insurance or assurance policy.

POOLED INVESTMENTS – often called 'collective investments' is money pooled together to buy a collection of stocks and shares. Unit Trusts and OEICs are typical examples.

PORTFOLIO – a collection of investments, such as shares, bonds, cash, or property. The process of buying or selling some of your investments is referred to as 'managing your portfolio'.

PRECIPICE BONDS – introduced in 1999, offering guaranteed high levels of income. But when stock markets fell, investors were upset when they received back only part of their original investment. ➜ INVESTMENTS

PREFERENCE SHARES – shares issued by companies, which normally pay a fixed rate of interest, before any dividends are paid on Ordinary Shares. Preference shares are less common these days. Companies now tend to issue corporate bonds. ➜ INVESTMENTS

PREMIUM – a sum paid to secure a benefit, in particular the amount paid for insurance/assurance.

PREMIUM BONDS – a very safe form of Government-backed gambling, because you never lose your initial stake and could win big tax-free cash prizes. ➜ SAVINGS

The name's Bond, Premium Bond

Premium Bonds hold a prize draw every month with a £1 million jackpot guaranteed – plus hundreds of thousands of other cash prizes.

Each £1 Bond has a separate and equal chance of winning a prize. The more Bonds you have, the better your chances of winning. As well as the £1 million jackpot you can win anything from £50 to £100,000 for each Bond you hold.

The table below gives an example of the number of prizes of each value for a prize fund of £40.1 million.*

Higher value: £1.6 million
(4 per cent of prize fund)

£1 million	1	£100,000	1
£50,000	3	£25,000	5
£10,000	11	£5,000	24

Medium value: £1.2 million
(3 per cent of prize fund)

£1,000	482	£500	1,146

Lower value: £37.3 million
(93 per cent of prize fund)

£100	1,729	£50	743,164

Total: £40.1 million

* Source: www.nsandi.com

Protection – more than just a safety belt

How would your family manage financially if you became seriously ill and couldn't work, or needed help to look after yourself? Have you ever wondered how your family would cope if you were to die unexpectedly? Amy Wringe of Scottish Widows offers options.

We all have hopes and dreams for the future, our children and the ones we love. And we work hard to provide for our family to help them become whatever they want to be in life. But we all have to face some startling facts. Here are just three:

Did you know?

- **We are 2 times more likely to suffer a critical illness than we are to die before the age of 60.**
  (Source: Taxbriefs – The Facts of Life and Health 2001)

- **Every 5 minutes in the UK, 6 people die.**
  (Source: www.financial-planning.uk.com, June 2003)

- **Over half of all deaths in the UK are caused by cancer, heart disease or cerebrovascular disease such as a stroke.**
  (Source: GE Frankona Re 2001)

If a crisis strikes

You may think that you will receive support from your employer. Although your employer may well provide sick pay, they're unlikely to provide you with the equivalent amount of salary you're currently earning. Furthermore, financial help from the State is almost non-existent and support services can be patchy depending on local resources.

This is where life and critical illness cover can help. It can help ensure that if you died unexpectedly or were diagnosed with a critical illness, your family would be financially provided for.

In the event that this ever happened:
- The plan will pay out a tax-free cash sum (under current rules).
- You may need to buy a new car that allows easy access for a wheelchair user.
- You may need to make alterations to your home.
- It could help pay for specialist medical treatment, perhaps only available outside the UK.

You may also find additional features in your plan, such as children's benefit. It is a common myth that children's cover is not needed because the illness would not affect the income of the main family bread-winner. However, the financial health of the family can depend on the physical health of all the family.

There may also be a guaranteed insurability option, which allows you to increase your original life insurance cover, for example up to twice its original amount, without further medical evidence. You can normally choose to activate this option if any of the following events happen to you; increasing your mortgage, the birth of a child, getting married or legally adopting a child.

Your plan can also be written in trust. The benefit of putting your plan under trust is that there is a quick payment to the people you have chosen as trustees and they can ensure a quick payment of proceeds to the people you have chosen as beneficiaries. It is also tax efficient as it is generally free of Inheritance Tax (based on current legislation).

Whilst money would never replace you, having adequate cover, for a serious illness or in the event of death, can be very important for your own peace of mind. It can also help your loved ones, should they ever need to make a claim.

SCOTTISH WIDOWS

Whatever life throws at you, make sure you're protected

Scottish Widows plc, registered in Scotland No.199549. Registered office in the UK at 69 Morrison Street, Edinburgh EH3 8YF. Telephone 0131 655 6000. Scottish Widows is a member of the Scottish Widows and Lloyds TSB Marketing Group, members of which carry on the business and services associated with life assurance, pensions and investments. Scottish Widows plc is authorised and regulated by the Financial Services Authority.

Money can't buy you
friends, but it can get you
a better class of enemy

Spike Milligan

PRE-NUPTIAL – an agreement between two people about to get married, often where one is much wealthier than the other and scared about losing a fortune if they should get divorced. Popular with older movie and rock stars. → DIVORCE for a word of warning.

PROBATE – When someone dies, an Executor has to obtain clearance to act before the assets can be transferred to those who will inherit. This process is normally called 'getting probate'. It makes sure that any inheritance tax due is assessed and paid out of the assets available, before the remaining assets are distributed in accordance with the Will.

PROTECTION – a favourite word both in sex education and insurance sales literature, only matched by 'safeguard' and 'peace of mind'.

PROXY – a person authorised to act for another.

PRUDENCE – is a virtue. It can mean not putting all your financial eggs in one basket.

PUBLIC LIABILITY – see *Liability*. → INSURANCE

PUBLIC LIMITED COMPANY (PLC) – a company whose shares are available to buy and sell on the stock market, but only if it is listed on the London Stock Exchange. See *Limited Company.*

QUALIFIED – Check that your adviser is qualified. → IFA

QUARTILE – basically another word for quarter, and a term often used when comparing investment funds. The best performing funds are in the top quartile.

QUID – a British pound. Not to be confused with 'quid pro quo', something which is given or done in return.

QUINS – five children born at the same time to the same mother. Not to be confused with the Harlequins rugby team, fifteen large men not born at the same time to the same mother. → CHILDREN

QUOTE (QUOTATION) – an indication of the amount that will be charged for a product or service, sometimes subject to conditions. A quote will be valid for a limited time for the person receiving the quote to accept within that specified period.

QUOTED COMPANY – a company that is listed on the Stock Exchange and whose shares the Quotations Committee has accepted.

R

REBATE – an amount returned when certain conditions have been met. As an example, an insurance policy might return part of the premium if there have been no claims, to discourage small claims. This would be a 'no claims rebate'.

RECESSION – Economists define a recession in terms of the rate of change in gross national product (GNP). When the rate of change in GNP is negative for two successive quarters, there is a recession.

REDEMPTION – paying off a mortgage, usually at the end of the term or when switching lenders.

REGULATED – The Financial Services Authority (FSA) is progressively pulling together all the rules that apply to personal financial services. In time, anyone offering such services will need to meet the FSA standards for training and conducting business.

REMORTGAGE – switching your mortgage from one lender to another without actually moving home. Competition in the market is fierce and it's increasingly common to 'test the market' every few years, seeking a cheaper mortgage. Those who hop around from one special rate to another are affectionately called 'rate tarts'.
→ MORTGAGES

REPAYMENT MORTGAGE – a mortgage where each month you pay some interest and some capital and the outstanding loan reduces over time.
→ MORTGAGES

RETIREMENT – The boundary between employment and retirement is less clear now than in the past, as a result of longer life expectancy, and the need for individuals to provide sufficient money to meet their needs and lifestyle.
→ ANNUITY, PENSIONS

RETIREMENT HOMES – from a condo in Florida to a semi in Southsea, properties that are designed to meet the needs of individuals and couples in their later years. More property developers are turning their attentions towards lower maintenance properties for this growing market.

RETURN – the amount by which an investment increases in value. This can be expressed as an income and/or growth.
→ INVESTMENTS

RICS – Royal Institution of Chartered Surveyors.

RIGHTS ISSUE – When a company needs to raise capital to boost dwindling funds, it may make a rights issue. If you're a shareholder, you are invited to buy new shares, normally at a discount to the current share value.

RIP – see *Funeral*.

RISK – Two individuals may regard the same risks differently, depending on the consequences. For example, the risk of losing £100 may be seen differently by an employee on the Minimum Wage and by a Company Director. It is generally believed that the greater the risk the greater the potential return. Also, a well-balanced investment portfolio can offset risk. ➔ INVESTMENTS

RPI – Inflation, or the tendency of prices to rise, is measured in the UK by the 'Retail Prices Index'. This official measure is calculated each month by taking a sample of goods and services that the typical household might buy.

RPI shopping basket – how times change

The Retail Prices Index is used to measure inflation in the UK, and is based on a 'shopping basket' of 650 goods and services on which we typically spend our money. The contents of this basket are updated each year, through the Office of National Statistics, based on a survey of consumer spending habits.

In 2004 for example, takeaway latte coffees, golf green fees, shower gel and powdered diet drinks all made it into the basket. Brown ale, cat litter, tinned spaghetti and vinyl flooring went out, reflecting changing tastes and spending patterns.

The basket of goods and services is kept fixed for a year at a time, so that from month to month the RPI only reflects changes in price. Government statisticians review the basket each year to keep it as up-to-date as possible. Items are dropped from the basket when they become more difficult to find in the shops or no longer typical of what most people spend their money on.

IN

- round lettuce
- diet-aid drink powder
- takeaway caffe latte
- takeaway kebab
- draught premium lager
- air fares
- designer spectacles
- hair and shower gel

Some changes in the RPI shopping basket for 2004

OUT

- brown ale
- man's belt
- battery powered clock
- electronic keyboard
- lead replacement petrol
- fixed telephone handset
- launderette
- dry cat food

For the full basket and how it's calculated, see National Statistics Online at www.statistics.gov.uk

S

SAVINGS – Why do we find saving so hard? ➔ *Feature*

S2P – State Second Pension. See *SERPS*.

SCHOOL FEES – If you're considering providing independent education for children, arrangements to cover the cost will be a significant issue. For fee levels and general guidance contact the Independent Schools Council Information Service.

SCORING (CREDIT) – a system used by lenders to determine 'good' and 'bad' risks. Different lenders have slightly different rules for assessing risk, but generally, answers you give on your application form will be given a rating. If the total 'score' is above a certain figure, your application is accepted.

SEARCHES – the investigations carried out on a property prior to the legal completion. The search checks local authority records, to see if any planning matters could cause future problems (such as a new motorway three streets away). The search also checks that the seller can in fact sell the property (has a clean title).

SECOND-HAND ENDOWMENTS – People who want to cash in an endowment policy generally have two options, to surrender it – hand it back to the life insurance company – or sell it in the second-hand market. Policyholders may get a higher price selling their policy than surrendering. The policy is assigned to the new investor, who will pay the monthly premiums and collect the full benefits at the end of the term. Speak to your IFA before making any rash decisions.

SECURED LOAN – a loan that requires some form of asset as security in case you default on repayments or skip the country. The security for a mortgage, for example, will be the property itself.

SECURITIES – a general term for any financial instrument traded on a stock exchange.

SERPS – The State Earnings Related Pension Scheme provides an additional pension to the basic state pension for employees with a record of sufficient earnings. In April 2002, the State Second Pension (S2P) superceded SERPS for new contributions.

Savings

How would you cope financially if you had to go without wages for a month or two? Squirrelling away some cash for emergencies is a good habit to get into. A savings plan is the first step towards a safer financial future and greater prosperity.

It depends on your financial situation, but setting aside a regular amount – say 10 per cent of your salary – will be a good starting point. Transferring this straight out of your pay packet into another account is a good idea. Just think of it as another bill that has to be paid and you'll be surprised how quickly you can build a lump sum.

Where to save?

There's plenty of choice of where to store your savings, but unlike investments, you are not presented with the same volume of decisions.

In building up a cash reserve, you probably want a low risk savings channel. Cash ISAs sold via banks and building societies work well.

With most ordinary savings accounts, you'll have to pay tax on any interest you earn. ISAs are a tax efficient storage facility, enabling you to save without paying tax on the growth of your savings, although there may be penalties for taking out your savings before the ISA has matured.

The ISA umbrella allows you to save up to £7,000 each tax year. There are currently two types – Mini and Maxi –

both of which let you hold a combination of investments depending on the level of risk you want to take.

Keep on saving

Even if you reach your annual ISA limit, you can continue saving free of tax using one of the National Savings and Investment plans. These include Savings Certificates, Premium Bonds and Children's Bonus Bonds.

Mini ISA	Maxi ISA
How many can you invest in?	
Three per year, but each must contain a different investment	Only one per year, and this has to be invested with one provider
What's the maximum investment amount?	
Overall maximum investment of £7,000 in any one tax year. There's an annual limit on each investment vehicle of: £3,000 in Cash ISA, £3,000 in Stocks and Shares ISA, £1,000 in Life Insurance ISA	£7,000 in a combination of stocks and shares, cash and insurance up to the limit
Can I choose different providers?	
Each Mini ISA can be sourced from a different provider	You can only choose one provider
Can I mix and match?	
You may only buy one of each investment type each year	You're not allowed to have both a Mini and Maxi ISA in the same financial year

Save the gap

The Government believes that we're not saving as much as we need to – the so-called 'savings gap'. Angus Maciver of Prudential explains the steps being taken to help consumers find their way through the financial fog, to bridge that gap.

Befuddled by finance?
If you're befuddled by finance or confused by credit, don't worry, you're not alone. Many of us just don't find the energy to decipher financial jargon or to understand how financial products work. As one result, many of us don't save enough or sometimes don't save at all. This helps to cause the 'savings gap'.

We want more
Many people in the UK find the financial industry difficult to understand. In fact, more than half (56 per cent) find it hard to understand financial leaflets and 57 per cent of consumers never, or hardly ever, read the personal financial pages of the newspapers. But it's our business to make a concerted effort to keep things plain and simple. Our latest Financial Literacy Survey shows that people *do* want to learn and understand more about financial issues and products that can affect their future security. In fact, 88 per cent believe there is a

need for *more* education and training in financial matters in the UK. What's more, 59 per cent feel that their education did not sufficiently prepare them to deal with their finances in adulthood.

> The majority of us want more financial education

Financial education programmes
Prudential has been involved in education programmes, aimed at delivering financial education to as wide an audience as possible, through the sponsorship of a variety of charities and independent organisations.

Our *Plan for Life Learning* programme is carried out in partnership with the Citizens Advice Bureau and various educational establishments. Together, we provide funding for nine centres to deliver face-to-face personal financial education to adults. A range of topics is covered – such as how to budget, saving, understanding credit and debt and financial planning.

The programme also supports more than 60 other bureaux already involved in financial education. It also provides sponsorship to other educational organisations, such as the National Institute of Adult and Continuing Education (NIACE), who offer a website learning resource, and the Personal Finance Education Group (PFEG), who focus on financial education in schools.

The industry watchdog, the Financial Services Authority (FSA), has been getting more involved in stepping up the pace of financial education in the UK. In recognition of our contribution to financial education, the FSA has asked us and others to help out.

And there is more
We launched *The Plan from The Pru* in September 2002. It's all about the way we help consumers think about their financial planning, develop products to suit, aim to provide excellent service and, most importantly, meet financial needs.

As part of the Plan, we offer a range of free, impartial, step-by-step guides to help you take control of your financial health. It's of vital importance that we all understand and feel comfortable with the financial products we buy. The best way to achieve this is through effective financial education.

PRUDENTIAL

For further details on *The Plan from The Pru*, please contact Prudential on 0800 000 000, visit www.prudential.co.uk or speak to your Sesame financial adviser.

SEVEN DEADLY SINS – Most of them apply to money and the desire for more.

PRIDE
GLUTTONY
LUST
ENVY
ANGER
SLOTH
COVETOUSNESS

SHARES – If you own shares in a company, you are entitled to vote at the Annual General Meeting and benefit from any dividends paid out of the company's profits. ➜ STOCKS AND SHARES

SHAREHOLDER – someone who owns Ordinary or Preference Shares in a company.

SHARE OPTIONS – Many companies have schemes for their employees and managers to buy shares in the company at a special price. There are many different types of scheme, but essentially, if the share price has gone up by the time you exercise the option, you can buy at the lower special price and sell the shares for a profit. With most company schemes like this you can't really lose, and could gain a lot.

SMP (Statutory Maternity Pay) – payment by the Government to cover a period of leave for 26 weeks just before and after having a baby. Many employers have

arrangements that are much more generous than SMP.

SOFA (The Society of Financial Advisers) – a leading professional and educational body for financial advisers. It is part of the Chartered Insurance Institute (CII) and boasts the largest number of members qualified to an advanced level in financial planning. ➜ CONTACTS

SOLICITORS – lawyers who typically provide a range of legal services, such as conveyancing, assistance with divorces and proceedings in the civil court, such as contract disputes and claims.

Q: How many personal injury lawyers does it take to change a light bulb?
A: Three – one to turn the bulb, one to shake him off the ladder and the third to sue the ladder company.

SPLIT CAPITAL INVESTMENT TRUSTS – better known as 'Splits', these trusts issue several types of shares. Some offer growth without income, others offer income without growth.

STAKEHOLDER PENSION – introduced in 2001 with low charges to encourage people on lower incomes to save for retirement. ➜ CHILDREN, PENSIONS

STAMP DUTY – a tax on certain financial transactions involving the transfer of assets, based on the capital value of the asset. The two most common examples are: Stamp Duty Land Tax that is payable

De-coding the newspaper columns

Market Capitalisation: the total shares multiplied by the share price, giving a total value the market puts on the company.

High/Low: the highest and lowest price in the last 12 months.

Dividend Yield: the last dividend paid as a percentage of the current share price.

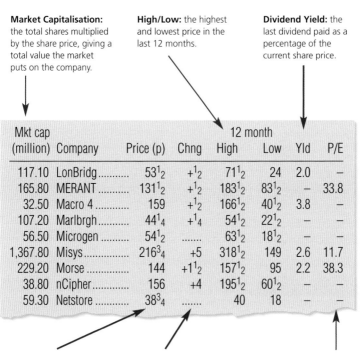

Mkt cap (million)	Company	Price (p)	Chng	12 month High	Low	Yld	P/E
117.10	LonBridg	$53\frac{1}{2}$	$+\frac{1}{2}$	$71\frac{1}{2}$	24	2.0	–
165.80	MERANT	$131\frac{1}{2}$	$+\frac{1}{2}$	$183\frac{1}{2}$	$83\frac{1}{2}$	–	33.8
32.50	Macro 4	159	$+\frac{1}{2}$	$166\frac{1}{2}$	$40\frac{1}{2}$	3.8	–
107.20	Marlbrgh	$44\frac{1}{4}$	$+\frac{1}{4}$	$54\frac{1}{2}$	$22\frac{1}{2}$	–	–
56.50	Microgen	$54\frac{1}{2}$	....	$63\frac{1}{2}$	$18\frac{1}{2}$	–	–
1,367.80	Misys	$216\frac{3}{4}$	+5	$318\frac{1}{2}$	149	2.6	11.7
229.20	Morse	144	$+1\frac{1}{2}$	$157\frac{1}{2}$	95	2.2	38.3
38.80	nCipher	156	+4	$195\frac{1}{2}$	$60\frac{1}{2}$	–	–
59.30	Netstore	$38\frac{3}{4}$	....	40	18	–	–

Price: the closing share price from the last trading day, in pence.

Change: the difference between the opening and closing price, either up (+) or down (-).

Price/Earnings (P/E) ratio: the share price, divided by the earnings per share (EPS). This ratio is a market judgement of the company's growth prospects. EPS is the net profit after tax divided by the total number of shares issued.

on the purchase of a house, which can be up to 4 per cent of the value of the house, dependent on amount; and Stamp Duty on the purchase of shares, which is 0.5 per cent of the amount paid.

STANDARD SECURITY – In Scotland this is the means by which lenders enforce their rights to a property if a borrower defaults on payments.

STATE PENSION ➜ PENSIONS

STATEMENT – a regular financial update used for bank accounts, pension schemes, an investment portfolio, or any other balance that can vary over time.

STATISTICS – 89 per cent of them are made up on the spot.

"There are three kinds of lies – lies, damned lies, and statistics."
Benjamin Disraeli

STOCK – a term used to describe the total capital of a company divided into shares. These days it's used interchangeably with shares. In the USA, shares are called stocks, which was how the phrase 'stocks and shares' came about.

STOCKBROKER – a trader who can give information, offer advice, sell and buy shares on behalf of clients. A key role of a stockbroker is to analyse stock performance and give recommendations ('buy', 'sell', 'hold'...).

STOCK MARKET – the market place for the sale and purchase of shares, bonds and Government securities.

STUDENT LOANS – a Government-sponsored arrangement that allows individuals in further education to borrow money through their period of study. On completion of the study, the loan becomes repayable depending on the individual's level of income. The interest arrangements are favourable during the period up to repayment, but then revert to normal loan interest rates.

SUMS INSURED – the total amount of money for which you are covered and the maximum an insurer will pay if your home is totally destroyed – say by fire or explosion. Your sums insured should be the amount it would cost to replace every item at today's prices.

SURRENDERING POLICIES – handing an endowment policy back to the life insurance provider. See also *Second-Hand Endowments*.

SURVEY – a check by the mortgage lender to make sure the property you are proposing to buy has been valued correctly. A basic valuation report is more for the lender's benefit than the buyer's, so if you want a more detailed inspection, ask for a full survey of the property. This will obviously cost you more, but can highlight any major structural defects like damp or subsidence.

Stocks and Shares

Over the long term, stocks and shares have performed better than other investments, like bonds and property, but are less secure. An investment in ordinary shares can produce an income, with dividends paid annually, but it may fluctuate. If the company's profits also grow, the share price can rise, which is called a capital gain. Not all companies grow and some don't pay dividends. The share price can also fall, and you may lose some or all of your investment.

How do I buy and sell shares?

You need to choose a stockbroker and set up an account. Internet trading is very popular, and you can be up and running in minutes. Other routes can take a few days. Technology has speeded up the process. Once you've got an account, you place an order, the shares are purchased and money is deducted from your account.

What are execution-only services?

These are brokers who, unlike traditional stockbrokers, don't give advice other than general market information. They simply act on your request to buy or sell shares. The service you choose depends on you:

• Are you confident making your own decisions or do you want advice?

• Do you want information at your disposal or are you happy to research it yourself?

• How do you want to deal with your broker – over the telephone, Internet or in person?

For serious investors, another option is to enrol the services of a discretionary portfolio broker. This broker has written authority to spend and invest money on your behalf. You and the portfolio manager usually agree on a set of goals and investment tactics, but all the day-to-day decisions are left to the manager, who'll report results at regular intervals. This isn't a service for your average investor, as these brokers are generally paid a significant fee. You also need to trust them completely.

Is there a minimum amount I can invest?

In reality, buying one share in a company isn't economic for you or them. Stockbrokers usually charge commission on each deal – subject to a typical minimum of £10–£25. The more hand holding you need, the greater the cost. You also have to pay stamp duty of 0.5 per cent on every share purchase.

That seems simple enough, what now?

There are many shares to choose from. You need to research the ones that are likely to provide a good return. The three broad categories are based on size:

Large Caps or 'Blue Chips' – well established companies, usually with a good track record for profits and increasing revenues.

Mid Caps – slightly riskier than 'blue chip' shares. Classified because the companies' market value is in the middle range.

Small Caps – Shares in small companies can be riskier still and are subject to rapid swings in value. Consequently gains and losses can be potentially greater than investing in larger companies.

Market sectors can react differently to economic conditions. The defence sector often benefits during a military crisis. Natural disasters like hurricanes and floods hit insurance companies hard. Keep informed of changes to the economy and watch the movements of prices. There's an array of investor publications, but for daily breakdowns read the share pages published in newspapers or running updates via the Internet or interactive TV.

Safe ways to start

Still wobbly on your feet? Then try some safer options to get you started. Fantasy investments are great confidence builders. Identify and research several companies, choosing an amount you might really invest then track the performance of these companies over a set period. Then look back and examine the winners and losers and how much your total portfolio grew.

Investment clubs are an alternative way to limit your risks. Join an existing one or set up your own with family and friends. You can contribute as little as £25 a month and share everything, including decision-making, financial knowledge and responsibility. Club membership can increase confidence and knowledge, with many members starting their own portfolio. Proshare (www.proshare.org) is one source of further information.

Many professionals make their living out of buying and selling shares, so you will need some luck to do better than the market. You will need to study, research and learn from successes and failures.

T

TARIFF – a statement of the rates charged for a service. Also, the duty or custom charges payable on import of goods.

TAX – Two things in life are certain (apart from death and taxes); tax avoidance is where accountants come into their own, and tax evasion can land you in jail.
→ TAX TIPS

TAX CODE – issued by the Inland Revenue to tell your employer how much tax to deduct from your pay. It's in your interest to make sure it's right. If you think your tax code may be wrong, you should tell your tax office straight away.

TAX EXILE – a person who leaves their country of birth to reduce their liability to tax.

TAX HAVEN – a country with low rates of tax, but often high rates of sunshine – except, perhaps, the Isle of Man.

TENANT – a person who rents a property. A tenancy agreement between a landlord and a tenant sets out the rights and obligations of both parties.

TERM – a period of time. Commonly used to describe the period over which a loan or mortgage will be repaid or for how long insurance cover will last.

TERM INSURANCE – life cover for a set number of years. A sum is only paid out if the life assured dies within the term specified. Otherwise there's no payout.
→ LIFE INSURANCE

TIED AGENT – an adviser who is only allowed to sell products from a particular supplier. Any adviser that is tied to one supplier has to make this clear, and not present themselves as giving advice based on an objective assessment of all the suppliers in the market place. ➜ IFA

TITLE – having the right of ownership.

TITLE DEEDS – In relation to property, these documents prove the right of ownership.

TOTAL RETURN – a combination of capital growth and reinvested income produced by an investment. This is normally quantified over a given period.

TRACKER – an investment fund that reproduces the make-up of a market index, such as the FTSE 100 index. Tracker funds are also referred to as passive investment funds. The aim is to achieve the same performance as the average investor, without the costs of an actively managed fund.

TRADED ENDOWMENT – an endowment policy that can be sold on to another person or institution. See *Second-Hand Endowments*.

TRADERS – dealers or organisations that operate in one of the financial markets to set up transactions between buyers and sellers. For shares, these are stockbrokers, but 'trader' is used in all financial markets.

TRANSFER VALUE – the amount of money available to transfer from one pension to another. Before deciding on transferring a pension, speak to your IFA, who can calculate whether this is the best use of these funds.

TRUST FUND – what every teenager hopes for on their 18th birthday. These are assets that are managed in accordance with a Trust Deed. Parents, or anyone else for that matter, can set up a trust. The aim is to transfer an asset in a way that ensures the beneficiary gets the assets and in a tax efficient way.

TRUSTEES – individuals who are appointed to administer a trust. Trustees are required to make decisions in the interest of the beneficiaries of the trust, and have unlimited personal liability for their actions. Trustees can be individuals or corporate trustees, whose directors have limited liability.

Tax Tips

Spend your allowance

Everyone, even children, has an annual personal tax allowance of £4,615 (2003/04) before income tax is due. There are larger allowances of £6,610 for anyone aged over 65, rising to £6,720 aged 75 and over. These may change at the start of each new tax year. If your spouse has no income, transfer savings and investments into his or her name.

Bare Essentials

- **The tax year runs from April to April.**

- **Many non-cash benefits from your employer will be taxed along with your salary, including healthcare schemes. Company cars are heavily taxed.**

- **Question carefully any advice to hold assets offshore to avoid UK tax. The Inland Revenue is constantly looking to close these tax loopholes.**

- **If you're self-employed, the deadline for tax due is 31st January each year. Forms can be completed online, or your accountant will file your return for a charge.**

- **Al Capone avoided arrest for his underworld crimes, but was jailed for evasion of taxes.**

As a couple, you'll then pay a lower rate of tax, if any at all, on savings. Check your tax code occasionally to make sure you're not paying more than necessary.

The ISA cherry

Individual Savings Accounts are a tax-efficient way to save, but have investment limits. → SAVINGS

Gifts from grandparents

Any income on money given to children by grandparents will use the child's personal allowance. Another 'all round' tax-efficient gift is a stakeholder pension for your grandchildren. Invest up to £2,808 a year and the Government adds 22 per cent, taking the maximum annual total to £3,600.

Capital Gains Tax

This tax on capital arises when an asset increases in value and is then sold or disposed of. Try to plan the timing of your sales to take advantage of the annual exemption, currently £7,900 per person. Married couples can transfer assets between them so both exemptions can be used. As with savings, it's always best to give the person in the lower tax bracket any taxable assets.

Avoiding tax by offsetting losses against gains is where the system gets more complicated. For example, if you've lost money on the stock market it may be prudent to carry the loss forward and offset it against any gains you make in future years. Your IFA can advise you on this.

Top up your pension pot

Making additional contributions to your pension within the Inland Revenue limits is very tax efficient. You can make AVCs – additional voluntary contributions – to a company pension scheme, normally up to 15 per cent of your earnings (including any mandatory contributions to the scheme). If you make a Personal Pension or Stakeholder Contribution, it can be up to 17.5 per cent of your income before age 35, which gradually grows to 40 per cent when you're 61 and over.

Claim your credits

Unlike allowances, which are automatic, you have to apply for tax credits. The Child Tax Credit is worth £543 off your tax bill each year and is available if you have a child under 16. The Working Tax Credit helps those in low paid work with families. It also includes the possibility of help towards childcare costs. Families on a joint income of up to £58,000 can claim. Ask the Inland Revenue if you think you qualify.

Working from home

If you run your business from home, you're entitled to claim a proportion of household expenses – heating, lighting and telephone calls – against your business expenses. These can be claimed through the self-assessment tax forms. Keep your household bills and calculate the amount as a proportion of the number of rooms used for business against the number of rooms in the house, but mind, you might lose part or all of the private residence exemption for capital gains tax on any part of the property used exclusively for business purposes.

Claim any expenses

Particularly relevant for the self-employed, make sure you keep any expenses receipts and claim them back. Tax isn't paid on expenses, which can include tools, travel and computers. If employed, make sure your employer reimburses you for travel and items you've paid for.

Inheritance Tax (IHT)

You can't take it with you, but ideally you'd like your assets to escape the clutches of the taxman, especially as anything over the £255,000 threshold is taxed at 40 per cent on death. Forward thinking is required here, especially if the value of your home now exceeds the Nil Rate Band. ➔ WILLS

Save with mortgage offsetting

Offsetting your mortgage against your savings and bank account is particularly attractive to higher-rate taxpayers. Firstly, you won't be taxed on any interest your savings earn. Also, because your mortgage is linked to credit balances, you only pay interest on the mortgage balance. But check the position with your mortgage lender.

You may not be able to avoid paying some tax but, with good advice, you can make the tax system work for you. Speak to your IFA.

U

UMBRELLA FUND – a collective investment to protect you when the sun is shining somewhere else. These funds are divided into a number of sub-funds, each investing in different assets and markets, so investors can shift their money to the most attractive sub-funds, sometimes at minimal cost. All umbrella funds are based in offshore centres like Jersey, Luxembourg and Dublin, and can't be operated in the UK, although many are recognised by the FSA.

UNAPPROVED PENSION SCHEMES – See *FURBS*.

UNDER INSURANCE – when the level of cover in an insurance policy is too small to meet a subsequent claim. It's vital to check your sums insured, to make sure you have adequate cover.

UNDERWRITERS – In insurance, underwriters are the people who determine the level of cover you receive in return for the agreed premium. In stock markets, when shares are offered for the first time in a market, underwriters are the people who charge a fee in return for agreeing to buy any shares that remain unsold.

UNIT-LINKED INVESTMENT – a financial product, the value of which is linked to the value of units of an investment fund. Examples are unit-linked endowment policies, pensions and annuities. **→ INVESTMENTS**

UNIT TRUST – a form of collective investment, which invests in a selection of shares and other assets, to create a portfolio. This portfolio is divided into individual units that can be bought and sold by investors. The performance of the unit trust will depend upon the selection made by the fund manager(s).
→ INVESTMENTS

UNLISTED SHARES – often applies to smaller companies, whose shares are not traded on any stock market. Companies are not quoted (or listed) because they prefer to run their business in private or they're too small to join a stock market.

V

VALUATION – the process of deciding what an item is worth, and in particular whether it is worth the price being asked. Valuations are normally undertaken by independent experts. Surveyors carry out house valuations for mortgage purposes.

VARIABLE RATE – the interest rate that a lender charges a borrower for a loan or mortgage. It follows the base rate, so can go up and down – as do your repayments. **➔ INTEREST RATES**

VAT (Value Added Tax) – tax collected on the sale of goods and services, which is administered in the UK by Customs and Excise. The standard rate of VAT in the UK is currently 17.5 per cent. Smaller organisations, below a threshold level, are not required to register for VAT.

VENDOR – another term for a seller.

VENTURE CAPITALISTS – organisations and individuals who invest in young companies, in the hope of realising large profits from their investment when the company is floated or sold.

VENTURE CAPITAL TRUSTS – companies listed on the stock market that invest in the shares of unlisted companies, or those on the AIM – Alternative Investment Market. These are available with certain tax advantages designed to persuade private investors to back small and fledgling enterprises. However, there are significant risks associated with investing in these types of companies.

VOLATILITY – the degree by which prices in a market or sector rise or fall.

VOLUNTARY EXCESS OR DEDUCTIBLE – a set amount of money, agreed in your insurance plan, which you agree to pay towards the cost of your claim. This may be applicable on each and every claim, or may be payable on the first claim over a given period of insurance. An excess or deductible (not standard excess) will usually result in lower premiums.
➔ INSURANCE

W

WAIVER – to let something pass. With Illness or Accident Insurance policies, the insurer may take over the monthly premium if you're ill or claiming benefit, to keep the insurance policy running during this period. By not insisting upon you paying the monthly premium, they are waiving it.

WALL STREET – the financial district in New York City, USA. In the 1980s movie 'Wall Street', the character Gordon Gekko (Michael Douglas) famously said: "Greed is good, greed is right, greed works".

WEALTH – the total value of all our assets less any liabilities or debt. Wealth can vary as the value of our assets (property, investments, savings) can go up and down, and as we pay back loans.

WEALTH CHECK – a systematic review of all the assets and liabilities for an individual or couple. Such checks are often undertaken by IFAs to identify any changes needed to help increase or protect your wealth.

WHOLE-OF-LIFE POLICY – a life insurance policy that will pay a death benefit no matter when you die. For most people it's not a necessity and you need to weigh up the fact that you'll be paying premiums for your lifetime.
➜ LIFE INSURANCE

WILLS – Where there's a Will there's a way to make sure your wishes get fulfiled when you're gone. ➜ *Feature*

WINDFALL – an unexpected good fortune. In recent years, customers of mutual building societies and insurance companies have received significant windfalls of shares when these companies converted to public limited companies. It's estimated that, during these conversions, nearly £20 billion was handed out.

WITH-PROFIT INVESTMENT – an investment tied to the performance of a fund. This type of investment usually applies to a pension, endowment, savings scheme or bonds. The idea is for fund managers to smooth out the rises and falls in the stock market by holding back profits in good years to help steady the overall performance in tougher years. The difficulty for an investor is that the future is always unknown and it's ▶112

What women want: a man's pension

Why can't a woman be more like a man? Abigail Morrison, of Standard Life, spells out the good and bad news for women when it comes to pensions. Government plans could help too.

The good news for women is that we're living longer than men*. A girl born in the UK in 1997 can expect to live to the ripe old age of 80, whereas for a boy it's 75*. So you might ask, is there any point in trying to be more like the boys?

In many respects, women tend to be better at looking after themselves than men. This translates into lower rates for

car and life insurance. But many women are not concerned enough about their financial well being in retirement until it's too late.

The bad news

On average, a woman retiring today will be poorer than her male colleague, for several reasons. First, because she's likely to live longer, any pension fund she has built up must last longer. This shows itself in lower annuity rates for women than for men.

The second problem is that women tend to earn less than men during their working lives– up to 37 per cent less in lifetime earnings. A woman's typical working pattern means she's more likely to take career breaks and to work part-time. Only 8 per cent of men work part-time, compared with 44 per cent of women*. Even when women work full-time, they're often more poorly paid than men. For example, in 1998 a woman's full-time hourly wage was, on average, 81 per cent of a man's*.

A final problem is that women often save less for their retirement than men. This is partly because they earn less, but also women in a relationship – especially those with children – seem to leave financial planning to their partners.

So women are triply challenged in building up a pension pot: compared with men, women live longer, they earn less and they save less.

> Compared with men, women live longer, earn less and save less

Flexibility is the answer

What can be done? Life expectancy is a fact of life, and the earnings gap between men and women seems unlikely to change significantly. Many women will continue to want career patterns that meet family needs, and would not choose otherwise.

So what's required is a flexible way to save. If the typical woman is going to stop and re-start working, reducing and increasing working hours as family circumstances change, she needs a pension plan that can cope.

Fortunately, help is at hand. Most modern pensions allow contributions to stop, start, and change with no penalty. Some companies even allow you to alter payments by a simple phone call.

The government proposals to simplify the rules on pensions will also make life easier for everyone saving for retirement. Instead of being restricted to annual pension savings of only 20 per cent to 25 per cent of earnings, everyone will be able to pay in the higher of 100 per cent of earnings or £3,600.

This will allow women to save more in their pension before they have children, to reduce payments during their children's younger years and then to make much larger contributions later to 'catch-up'.

The government's new proposals mean that women will have more options than ever when it comes to saving for retirement. But one fact will remain: when it comes to pensions, a woman is not like a man, and must look after her own interests if she wants to secure a comfortable retirement.

STANDARD LIFE

* Source: FSA Consumer Research Report: Women and Personal Finance: the reality of the gender gap (April 2001)

Note: Tax and legislation are likely to change. The information given here is based on Standard Life's understanding of law and Inland Revenue practice at the date of publication.

Wills

Writing a Will needn't be a headache or a costly exercise. Even so, two-thirds of the population fails to make one. Whatever stage you are at in life, you owe it to your next of kin to set your wishes straight.

Can I write my own Will?

If you have just basic requests, it's not rocket science. You can buy a pre-printed form from the Internet or high street stationers, although it's much safer to seek a solicitor's expertise – who will include clear, specific instructions. Simply list all your assets and ask a solicitor to translate it into an official document. If you use a solicitor, a Will for an individual can cost as little as £70 to draft, but prices will vary depending on the solicitors you use and the complexity of your requirements. It's a good idea to ask for an estimate so you know what you can expect to pay.

You will also need to appoint an executor – someone you trust, or a solicitor or bank (who will charge a fee for the service). The executor will carry out your wishes.

What makes a Will valid?

It must be signed by the person making the Will, and witnessed by two persons (only one witness required in Scotland) – not people who'll benefit from the Will.

What must I say in my Will?

It's important to state that this Will revokes all others – even if you haven't made one before. This makes clear there is no other Will, hopefully preventing major family disputes. It also needs to state:

- the executors
- the people you want to benefit with their full name and relationship to you
- specific instructions for particular possessions
- guardians for your children until they are 18.

How often should I update it?

Wills need to be reviewed regularly, especially if your personal circumstances change. It definitely needs changing if you:

- get married or re-married
- get divorced (although divorce doesn't automatically make a Will invalid)
- want to make large alterations to the original.

Can I make changes on the original?

No, any alterations to the original document will not be valid unless they're done officially. This doesn't mean completely re-drafting, but you need to instruct a solicitor to make a codicil – the official name for a supplementary change. Any major changes are better made through a new Will.

What if I have my own business?

A Will is vital in these circumstances and you need to make clear what you want to happen to your share of the business. It's important your personal Will doesn't conflict with any business partnership agreement. Seek specialist advice and advise your business partners to do the same.

What does 'intestate' mean?

This means to die without a Will. If you've not left any instructions and leave less than £125,000, your current spouse inherits everything – even stepchildren, un-married partners and your children will have no provision.

If you're married with no children, your spouse inherits the first £200,000 and personal possessions and one half of the rest. The other half is divided between your parents and nearest relatives.

If you're unmarried, and have no close relatives, your estate could go to a distant relative or even the Government. Even partners you've lived with for years are not entitled to anything.

Are there ways to limit the amount of potential Inheritance Tax liability?

If you have a lot of assets, your heirs may be faced with a hefty tax bill. Inheritance Tax (IHT) is set at 40 per cent on the total value of assets over a certain amount (£255,000 in 2003/04). As house prices have risen, more individuals have assets worth more than this threshold. For married couples, assets can pass from the first to die to the surviving spouse without tax being payable, but this only delays the potential tax liability. Fortunately, there are some ways to reduce the amount of IHT payable.

Assets can be distributed during your lifetime by gifts to relatives and friends, but you have to survive for seven years after making the gift to exclude it from your estate. So, don't leave it too late. Small gifts – up to an annual limit of £3,000 – are exempt from the seven-year rule, as are certain other transfers – for example donations to UK registered charities.

An alternative is placing your assets into trusts, for the benefit of your children, grandchildren, or other worthy causes. The law related to trust property is complex, so seek advice from your IFA or a solicitor.

Since your home is likely to be your largest asset, a married couple should also seek advice on the most tax-efficient way of owning the property between them. Many couples are moving from ownership by 'joint tenancy' to being 'tenants in common'. If you've not looked at this possibility, consult your IFA, who can explain the ins and outs.

You might want to keep the contents of your Will secret – but let a few people know where it's stored.

If no one can find it, what was the point in writing one?

hard to predict the overall performance. That's why many investors prefer unit trusts, as it's easier to track the performance of your investments.

WOMEN SPECIALISTS – Although most financial products are unisex, many advisers and insurers see women as a niche area. There are now specialist motor insurers who cater solely for women, rewarding careful drivers with lower premiums. There are even women-only breakdown recovery policies. Pensions are also an issue, with many women taking time out from work to raise a family.

WORKING TAX CREDIT – a tax incentive for people in low-paid work. The system of tax credits changed in April 2003, introducing the new Child Tax Credit and the new Working Tax Credit to encourage people to take a job. Usually administered by employers, to qualify for Working Tax Credit there are certain conditions, including:
• Working 16 hours or more a week
• Being paid for that work
• Expecting to work for at least four weeks.
For full details and to check your entitlements, telephone 0845 300 3900 or go online at www.inlandrevenue.gov.uk/taxcredits.
➜ CHILDREN, CONTACTS

WRITE OFF – when vehicles are sent to the big scrap yard in the sky. If your car is involved in an accident, the insurer will look at the value of the car against the cost of getting it repaired. For example, if your car is only worth £500 but repairs will cost £1,000, it's not worth paying to get it back on the road. Insurers will call this a write-off, and either settle with cash or provide a replacement vehicle.

XY&Z

XD – EX-DIVIDEND – the period of time between the announcement of a dividend and the payment to shareholders. For transactions during the ex-dividend period it is the seller, not the buyer, who will receive the dividend. Ex-dividend is usually indicated in newspapers with an x next to the stock's name.

YACHT – normally comes after the large new house and sports car, but before the private jet.

YIELD – an alternative word for return. This is the amount that an investment earns, expressed as a percentage of the amount put in, or of its market value.

ZERO-RATED – Certain goods and services are subject to Value Added Tax, but the rate is zero. Organisations, that make zero-rated supplies have to account for the tax to Customs and Excise, but no VAT is collected from the buyer.

Contacts

Advice UK
Previously called the
Federation of Information and
Advice Centres
12th Floor
New London Bridge House
25 London Bridge Street
London SE1 9ST
Tel: 020 7407 4070
www.adviceuk.org.uk

**Association of Independent
Financial Advisers (AIFA)**
Austin Friars House
2–6 Austin Friars
London EC2N 2HD
Tel: 020 7628 1287
Fax: 020 7628 1678
www.aifa.net

**Association of British Credit
Unions (ABCUL)**
Holyoake House
Hanover Street
Manchester M60 0AS
Tel: 0161 832 3694
www.abcul.org

**Association of British
Insurers (ABI)**
51 Gresham Street
London EC2V 7HQ
Tel: 020 7600 3333
www.abi.org.uk

**Banking Code Standards
Board**
33 St James's Square
London SW1Y 4JS
Tel: 020 7661 9694
www.bankingcode.org.uk

British Bankers' Association
Pinners Hall
105–108 Old Broad Street
London EC2N 1EX
Tel: 020 7216 8800
www.bba.org.uk

**Building Societies
Association**
3 Savile Row
London W1S 3PB
Tel: 020 7437 0655 – ask for
BSA Consumer Line
www.bsa.org.uk

**Citizens Advice Bureau
Service (CAB)**
Myddelton House
115–123 Pentonville Road
London N1 9LZ
www.adviceguide.org.uk

**Council for Mortgage
Lenders (CML)**
3 Savile Row
London W1X 1AF
Tel: 020 7437 0655
www.cml.org.uk

**Consumer Credit
Counselling Service (CCCS)**
Wade House
Merrion Centre
Leeds LS2 8NG
Tel: 0800 138 1111
www.cccs.co.uk

Consumer Gateway
An online source of
comprehensive consumer
information from the
Department of Trade and
Industry (DTI)
www.dti.gov.uk/
consumer_web

Consumers' Association
2 Marylebone Road
London NW1 4DF
Tel: 0845 307 4000
www.which.net

Experian
Consumer Help Service
Experian Limited
PO Box 8000
Nottingham NG1 5GX
Tel: 0870 241 6212
www.experian.co.uk

**Financial Ombudsman
Service**
South Quay Plaza
183 Marsh Wall
London E14 9SR
Tel: 0845 080 1800
www.financial-
ombudsman.org.uk

Financial Services Authority (FSA)
25 The North Colonnade
Canary Wharf
London E14 5HS
Helpline: 0845 606 1234
www.fsa.gov.uk/consumer

Financial Services Compensation Scheme
7th Floor Lloyds Chambers
Portsoken Street
London E1 8BN
Helpline: 020 7892 7300
www.fscs.org.uk

General Insurance Standards Council (GISC)
110 Cannon Street
London EC4N 6EU
Tel: 0845 601 2857 (calls charged at local rate) or
020 7648 7800
www.gisc.co.uk

HM Customs and Excise
For general written enquires write to:
Customer Focus Team
Business Services and Taxes
New Kings Beam House
22 Upper Ground
London SE1 9PJ
Tel: 0845 010 9000
(National Advice Service)
www.hmce.gov.uk

Independent Banking Advisory Service
Somersham
Huntingdon
Cambridgeshire PE28 3WD
Helpline: 01487 843444
www.ibas.co.uk

Inland Revenue
www.inlandrevenue.gov.uk

Money Advice Trust
Bridge House
181 Queen Victoria Street
London EC4V 4DZ
Tel: 020 7489 7796
www.moneyadvicetrust.org

National Debtline
The Arch
48–52 Floodgate Street
Birmingham B5 5SL
Freephone: 0808 808 4000
www.nationaldebtline.co.uk

Occupational Pensions Regulatory Authority (OPRA)
Invicta House, Trafalgar Place
Brighton
East Sussex BN1 4DW
Tel: 01273 627600
www.opra.gov.uk

Office of Fair Trading (OFT)
Fleetbank House
2–6 Salisbury Square
London EC4Y 8JX
Tel: 08457 22 44 99
www.oft.gov.uk

The Pensions Advisory Service (OPAS)
11 Belgrave Road
London SW1V 1RB
Tel: 0845 601 2923
www.opas.org.uk

Pensions Ombudsman
11 Belgrave Road
London SW1V 1RB
Tel: 020 7834 9144
www.pensions-ombudsman.org.uk

Sesame
Oasis Park
Stanton Harcourt Road
Eynsham
Oxon OX29 4AE
Tel: 01865 886000
www.sesame.co.uk

Society of Financial Advisers (SOFA)
20 Aldermanbury
London EC2V 7HY
Tel: 020 7417 4442
www.sofa.org

Abbey

To find out more about Abbey products and services for individuals visit the 'Find an Adviser' area at www.sesame.co.uk to find your nearest Sesame Financial Adviser.

Abbey is the sixth largest bank by assets in the UK, the 16th largest in Europe, and the 30th largest in the world. We're the second largest provider of mortgages and savings in the UK and provides personal financial products and services including mortgages, savings, investments, banking, general insurance and life assurance.

Abbey for Intermediaries encompasses Abbey National's intermediary facing business – James Hay, Cater Allen, Scottish Mutual (UK and International) and Scottish Provident (UK and International).

www.abbey.com

AXA

AXA is a world leader in financial protection and wealth management, with major operations in Western Europe, North America and the Asia/Pacific area. As of 31 December 2003, AXA had €775 billion in assets under management.

Telephone 0117 989 3000

As part of our commitment to quality service, phone calls may be recorded.

www.axa.co.uk

Prudential

For more than 150 years Prudential's business has been guided by its founding principles of integrity and security.

Over the last century Prudential has expanded internationally and broadened its product range, and now is a leading provider of retail financial products and fund management, with operations in the UK and Europe, the US and Asia.

Prudential's product range includes:

- Annuities
- Car/Home/Travel Insurance
- Equity Release
- High Interest Deposit Accounts
- 60-day Notice Accounts
- Mortgages
- ISA, PEP and Unit Trust Investments
- Personal Pension Plans
- Prudence Family Cover
- Prudence Critical Illness Cover
- Mortgage Protection Plans
- Low Cost Endowments
- Life Plans
- Prudential Investment Bonds
- Prudence Savings Accounts

Prudential plc
Pountney Hill
London EC4R 0HH

Telephone 0800 000 000 or 020 7220 7588

www.prudential.co.uk
www.pru.co.uk

PRUDENTIAL

Scottish Widows

Scottish Widows has been working to help people plan their financial futures since its formation as Scotland's first mutual life office in 1815. Since then the company has gone from strength to strength and is now one of the most recognised brands in the life, pensions and investment industry*

Scottish Widows' vision is to be the best life, pensions and investment company in the UK. It's product range includes ordinary long term insurance - such as life assurance, pensions, annuities and permanent health insurance - and savings and investment products.

Scottish Widows plc
69 Morrison Street
Edinburgh EH3 8YF

Telephone 0845 608 0371

www.scottishwidows.co.uk

*Source: MarketMinder to June 2003

Standard Life

Standard Life has been successfully looking after its customers for more than 175 years, and currently over 5 million people rely on us for their financial needs.

Our mutual status is one of the key reasons for our success. As we do not have shareholders to satisfy we can focus solely on meeting customers' needs.

Standard Life has the financial strength to remain secure and competitive. We offer products that allow us to remain financially secure while at the same time giving competitive returns to customers.

The Standard Life Group offers the following:

- Pensions
- Savings
- Protection
- Life Assurance
- Investments
- Banking
- Healthcare

Standard Life
Standard Life House
30 Lothian Road
Edinburgh EH1 2DH

Telephone 0131 225 2552

www.standardlife.co.uk

Zurich

To find out more about Zurich's products and services, please speak to your Independent Financial Adviser (IFA). If you don't have an IFA you can search for one in your area by logging on to www.unbiased.co.uk.

Zurich Financial Services is an insurance-based financial services provider with an international network that focuses its activities on its key markets of North America, the UK and Continental Europe. Founded in 1872, Zurich is headquartered in Zurich, Switzerland. It has offices in more than 50 countries and employs approximately 64,000 people.

Basing its business on a tradition of innovative financial solutions, Zurich is one of the world's major players in insurance and offers its customers a comprehensive range of insurance products - such as property, travel and car insurance as well as financial products such as life cover, investment and pensions.

Zurich is a top-five player in most of its markets and leads the way in many.

www.zurich.com